ORTHODOX ICONOGRAPHY

St. John the Theologian and his disciple St. Prochoros. 1345.
Miniature in a manuscript Book of the Gospels, Monastery of
St. John the Theologian, Patmos.

ORTHODOX ICONOGRAPHY

Four essays dealing with the History of Orthodox Iconography, the Iconographic Decoration of Churches, the Functions of Icons, and the Theology and Aesthetics of Byzantine Iconography. In addition, three Appendixes containing Authoritative Early Christian Texts on Icons, explanations of the Techniques of Iconography, and a discussion of Two Russian Books on Icons

BY

CONSTANTINE CAVARNOS

INSTITUTE FOR BYZANTINE
AND MODERN GREEK STUDIES
115 Gilbert Road
Belmont, Massachusetts 02178
U.S.A.

PREFACE

The texts that make up the present volume were written at different times, and without the idea of constituting this book. I have brought them here together in order to make them available in a more useful form. They deal with various aspects of one and the same subject, and present a fairly comprehensive, even though brief, discussion of the topic of holy icons from the standpoint of Eastern Orthodox Christianity.

Chapters 1 and 2, "Brief History of Iconography" and "Iconographic Decoration of Churches," are revised versions of the main part of the study "Iconographic Decoration in the Orthodox Church," which I contributed to *The Orthodox Ethos*. This is a book that was edited by Dr. A. J. Philippou and printed in 1964 at Oxford by Holywell Press Ltd. for the Greek Orthodox Archdiocese of North and South America. Chapter 3, "The Functions of Icons," is a paper which I read at a Symposium on Iconography held at the Church of St. Nicholas at Lexington, Massachusetts, on November 9, 1975. It appears in print for the first time. The fourth chapter, "Theology and Aesthetics of Byzantine Iconography," is the greater part of my article "Byzantine Iconography," which was published in the January-June, 1972 issue of the Athenian journal *Theologia*. The "Two Authoritative Early Christian Texts Concerning Holy Icons" that make up Appendix A have appeared in my pamphlet, *The Icon: Its Spiritual Basis and Purpose*, which was first published in 1955 at Haverhill, Massachusetts, by The Byzantine Publishers, and has since then been reprinted twice by the Institute for Byzantine and Modern Greek Studies. Appendix B, "The Techniques of Iconography by Photios Kontoglou," consists of translations which I have made from some publications of this eminent painter and writer. They appear in English for the first time, and are intended to give the reader a general idea of how icons are made. Appendix C, "Two Russian Books on Icons," consists of my reviews of Eugene N. Trubetskoi's *Icons: Theology in Color,* and of Leonide Ouspensky's and Vladimir Lossky's *The Meaning of Icons.* The first was published in the Autumn, 1974 issue of *The Greek Orthodox Theological Review,* and is reprinted here without changes; the second appeared in the July, 1957 issue of *Speculum,* and is reprinted in revised form.

In order to illustrate some of the chief points of these texts and help the reader acquire a more definite notion of Orthodox iconography, I have included twenty-five plates, showing some of the finest works of this tradition — mosaics, wall paintings, panel icons, and miniatures — and some of their settings: a *proskynetarion,* an iconostasis, an apse, a dome.

I am very grateful to the publisher of the *Orthodox Ethos,* and to the editors of the above mentioned journals for permission to reprint the respective texts which appeared in them. I also owe many thanks to my iconographer friend Mr. Demetrios Dukas, for having gone over the entire manuscript and made many helpful comments, and to my former colleague Professor J. Arthur Martin of Wheaton College (Mass.), for reading the chapter "Theology and Aesthetics of Byzantine Iconography" and suggesting many improvements in expression.

CONSTANTINE CAVARNOS

March, 1977

CONTENTS

PREFACE vii

LIST OF ILLUSTRATIONS xi

I BRIEF HISTORY OF ICONOGRAPHY 13

II ICONOGRAPHIC DECORATION OF CHURCHES 22

III THE FUNCTIONS OF ICONS 30

IV THEOLOGY AND AESTHETICS OF
BYZANTINE ICONOGRAPHY 36

APPENDIX A:
TWO AUTHORITATIVE EARLY CHRISTIAN TEXTS
1. ST. JOHN DAMASCENE 49
2. THE SEVENTH ECUMENICAL SYNOD 51

APPENDIX B:
THE TECHNIQUES OF ICONOGRAPHY
BY PHOTIOS KONTOGLOU 55

APPENDIX C:
TWO RUSSIAN BOOKS ON ICONS
1. *ICONS: THEOLOGY IN COLOR* 60
2. *THE MEANING OF ICONS* 63

BIBLIOGRAPHY 67

INDEX 69

ILLUSTRATIONS

Plate

St. John the Theologian and his disciple St. Prochoros. 1345. Miniature in a manuscript, Patmos. *Frontispiece.*

1. Proskynetarion. 1779. Church of the Transfiguration at Megalochorion, Lesbos.

2. Iconostasis. Chapel of the Three Great Hierarchs, Monastery of Barlaam, Meteora.

3. The Theotokos as *Platytera* and the Child Christ. *Ca.* 1950. Fresco by Photios Kontoglou, Church of Kapnikarea, Athens.

4. The Theotokos as *Hodegetria* and the Child Christ. XIIth century. Mosaic, Monastery of St. Catherine, Mount Sinai.

5. The Theotokos as *Glykophilousa.* 1955. Panel icon by Photios Kontoglou.

6. Christ the Pantocrator. XIVth century. Panel icon, Church of St. Therapon, Mytilene.

7. Christ the Merciful. 1952. Panel icon by Photios Kontoglou, Church of St. Euthymios, Piraeus.

8. St. John the Baptist. XVIth century. Panel icon, Church of the Protaton, Mount Athos.

9. St. Paul the Apostle. Detail. Early XVth century. Panel icon by Andrew Rublev.

10. Christ the Pantocrator. *Ca.* 1100. Mosaic in the dome, Church of Daphni, near Athens.

11. Fully decorated dome. 1957. Frescoes by Photios Kontoglou and his assistants, Church of St. Nicholas at Kato Patesia, Athens.

12. The Prophet Jeremiah. 1972. Mosaic by Demetrios Dukas, Church of the Holy Wisdom (*Hagia Sophia*) at Washington, D.C.

xi

13. St. Luke the Evangelist. Detail. 1971. Mosaic by Demetrios Dukas, Church of the Holy Wisdom, Washington, D.C.

14. The Nativity. 1462. Wall painting, Church of the Holy Cross at Agiasmati, Cyprus.

15. The Baptism of Christ. Xth century. Miniature in a manuscript, Monastery of Iviron, Mount Athos.

16. The Crucifixion. XIth century. Mosaic, Church of the Monastery of Hosios Lukas, Boeotia.

17. The Resurrection. XIth century. Mosaic, Church of Hosios Lukas.

18. The Ascension. *Ca.* 1950. Fresco by Photios Kontoglou, Church of Zoodochos Pighi at Liopesi (Paiania), Attica.

19. Group of Martyrs in prayer. XIVth century. Fresco, Church of Aphentiko or Brontocheiou, Mystra.

20. St. George the Great Martyr. Probably XVIIth century. Panel icon, Church of St. Symeon, Mytilene.

21. The Prophet Zacharias. Detail from the Presentation of the All-Holy Virgin. XIVth century. Fresco by Manuel Panselinos, Church of the Protaton, Mount Athos.

22. St. Symeon Nemanya. 1314. Fresco, Church of Studenitza, Yugoslavia.

23. Three Angels. Depiction known as the Holy Trinity. *Ca.* 1411. Panel icon by Andrew Rublev, Tretiakov Gallery, Moscow.

24. Sts. Euthymios and Savvas. 1535. Fresco by Theophanes the Cretan, main church of the Monastery of Lavra, Mount Athos.

CHAPTER I

BRIEF HISTORY OF ICONOGRAPHY

The Greek word *eikon,* from which the English term *icon* is derived, means 'likeness,' 'image,' 'representation.' The use of icons by Christians goes back to the first century. A rudimentary symbolic art existed among the Christians of the first two centuries, employing such forms as the Dove (symbol of the peace of Christ), the Fish and the Shepherd (symbols of Christ), and the Peacock (symbol of the resurrection). Further, it seems that as early as the first century Christians used representations of events in Holy Scripture to decorate their tombs; and pictorial representations of events from the life of Christ, probably dating from the early part of the second century, have been found in catacombs at Rome and Alexandria. Pictorial representations increase with each century, until the outbreak of Iconoclasm in 726.

Christian writers of the first few centuries testify to the existence of sacred icons in their time, and stress the value which icons have for the Christian. Thus, St. Basil the Great (*c.* 330–379), in his homily on the martyrdom of Barlaam, says: "Arise now before me, you iconographers of the deeds of the saints. . . . Let me be overwhelmed by your icons depicting the brave acts of the martyr! Let me look at the fighter most vividly depicted in your icon. . . . Let also Christ, Who instituted the contest, be depicted in your icon."[1] In a fragment of a *Life of St. John Chrysostom* (*c.* 347–407), preserved in a work by St. John Damascene (*c.* 675–749), we are told that Chrysostom had an icon of the Apostle Paul before himself as he studied Paul's Epistles. When he looked up from the text, the icon seemed to come to life and speak to him.[2] Damascene

---

[1] Migne, *Patrologia Graeca,* Vol. 31, col. 489a–c. Henceforth I shall refer to this work as *P.G.*

[2] *P.G.,* Vol. 94, col. 1277c.

also tells us that Chrysostom was fond of another icon, too, which was marked by its holiness. "In it," he says, "I saw depicted an angel putting the hosts of the barbarians to flight, and David prophesying truly: Lord, Thou shalt cause their image to vanish out of the city."[3] And St. Gregory of Nyssa (c. 330–395) tells us how deeply he was moved by an icon of the sacrifice of Isaac: "I have often beheld a painted representation of the passion, and have never passed by this sight without shedding tears, for art brings the story vividly to the eyes."[4]

With each succeeding century the number and variety of pictorial representations increases, and iconography becomes more and more mature and stylized. The style of painting known as Byzantine may be said to date from the sixth century. Various influences contributed to its formation. The three most important were: the Hellenic, the Oriental (mainly Syrian), and the Christian. To Greece this art owes its idealism, its clarity, elegance, and balance. From Syria it received a vigorous expressionism, achieved through the use of frontal poses, the markedly disproportionate enlargement of the eyes and head, and a similar enlargement of the principal personages in relation to those about them. These elements of idealism and vigorous expression were fused together, the one sometimes predominating over the other, by the Christian faith. The doctrines of the Christian Church set the limits within which iconography should operate, while the inner living faith of the icon painter, expressing itself through the material media, utilized these and other elements to convey the facts, truths, and values of the Christian religion. It is this third factor, more than anything else, that has given Byzantine iconography its distinctive character as an art of the highest spirituality.

The fusion of these three factors — the Hellenic, the Oriental, and the Christian — which gave rise to the Byzantine style, took place primarily in the capital of the Byzantine Empire, Constantinople. From here this style spread to Asia Minor, the whole Balkan Peninsula (present day Greece, Yugoslavia, Bulgaria, Rumania), Italy, Russia, and more distant countries.

---

3   *Ibid.*, cols. 1313b, 1400c.
4   *Ibid.*, col. 1269c.

The iconoclastic ban on icons interrupted the development of iconography in Byzantium for more than a century (726–843) and caused a large-scale destruction of icons in the Empire. In Constantinople, where the ban was most sternly enforced, panels were entirely forbidden, while mosaics and wall paintings were restricted to ornamental works and symbols like the cross. Representation of the human form in churches was forbidden by the rulers. There resulted from this a great loss in the churches' uplifting power and mystical charm. Speaking about the great church of Hagia Sophia at Constantinople some years after the end of Iconoclasm, the Ecumenical Patriarch Photios (*c.* 810–895) remarked that "this celebrated and sacred church looked sad with its visual mysteries scraped off, as it were. . . ." [5]

With the downfall of Iconoclasm in the middle of the ninth century, iconography began to develop with great vigor and system. Mainly from the following century, a definite order for the arrangement of icons in the church became established in the Christian East, and has continued, with certain variations from period to period, down to the present. The arrangement was dictated by functional aims.

The first important iconographic decorations of churches were mosaics. Christians borrowed the art of mosaics from the Greeks and Romans, who had used it chiefly for pavements. Use was now made of this technique for decorating the walls, vaults, apses and domes of churches with sacred figures and events.

Among the oldest surviving churches with mural mosaics are Hosios David and St. George at Thessaloniki, which both have mosaics done in the fifth century; and the Mausoleum of Galla Placidia and the Baptistery of the Orthodox at Ravenna, whose mosaics also date from the fifth century. Among those next in antiquity are the mosaics of Sant' Apollinare Nuovo, Sant' Apollinare in Classe and San Vitale at Ravenna, and Sts. Cosmas and Damian at Rome (sixth century); St. Demetrios and Hagia Sophia at Thessaloniki (seventh, and eighth and ninth centuries respectively); Hagia Sophia at Constantinople (latter part of the

---

[5] Cyril Mango, ed. and trans., *The Homilies of Photius, Patriarch of Constantinople,* Cambridge, Mass., 1958, p. 292.

ninth century and later); Nea Moni in Chios, Hosios Lukas in
Boeotia, and Daphni near Athens (eleventh century); and the Holy
Apostles at Thessaloniki and the Monastery of Chora (Kahrie
Djami) at Constantinople (fourteenth century).

Mosaics were extensively used in the Byzantine Empire from
the fourth to the fourteenth centuries. During this period they were
of primary importance in church decoration. Iconoclasm interrupted iconographic decoration, as we have said, for more than a
century. The first major mosaic decoration after the defeat of Iconoclasm was completed in 867. It was a representation of the All-
Holy Virgin (*Panagia*) and Child in the Church of Hagia Sophia
at Constantinople. After the fourteenth century, the impoverished
condition of the Empire, resulting from the Crusades from the West
on the one hand, and the repeated attacks of the Ottoman Turks
from the East on the other, made mosaic decoration of churches
virtually impossible. Less costly means had to be employed. The
Byzantines made use of frescoes — murals executed with pigments
mixed with water and applied on moist plaster. In recent years, the
employment of mosaics for iconographic decoration has been re-
vived, though on a small scale, in Greece, the United States and
elsewhere.

The use of mosaics has not been restricted to wall decoration,
although this has been their primary use. They have also been
employed on panels, sometimes of extremely small dimensions. A
certain number of miniature mosaics on panels, as well as some
larger ones, of the same size as the icons which are mounted upon
the lower part of the iconostasis, have survived in some of the
monasteries on Mount Athos[6] and in a few other places. Their
dates vary from the twelfth to the fourteenth centuries.

The methods of iconographic decoration by mosaics and by
frescoes have not been regarded as mutually exclusive: often we see
both kinds of decoration in the same church. But mosaics have been
considered the superior mode of iconography.

We have already noted that wall paintings were used at a very

---

6   See my book *Anchored in God: Life, Art, and Thought on the Holy
Mountain of Athos,* Athens, 1959, Belmont, Mass., 1975, pp. 67, 85, 143, 153–
154, 218.

early date in the catacombs. The earliest examples which survive
are in the catacombs of Rome. Among the oldest surviving frescoes
in churches are those at Dura, Syria, done shortly before 250.
Important mural paintings of an early date also survive at Baouit,
Saqqara, and elsewhere in Egypt (fifth century); in the church of
Santa Maria Antiqua at Rome (eighth and ninth centuries); and
elsewhere. Not as old, but of considerable importance, are the
monastic mural paintings of Cappadocia (between the ninth and
the eleventh centuries).

Countless wall paintings of high merit survive in the Orthodox
countries: Greece, Yugoslavia, Bulgaria, Rumania, Russia. Greece
and Yugoslavia have the largest number of such icons. In Greece,
the most numerous frescoes and some of the best are to be seen in
churches in Attica (tenth to eighteenth centuries), Mystra (fourteenth and fifteenth centuries), Mount Athos and Kastoria (fourteenth, fifteenth, and sixteenth centuries), and Meteora (sixteenth
and seventeenth centuries). In Yugoslavia, remarkable frescoes are
to be seen in the cathedral of Hagia Sophia at Ochrida (eleventh
century) and in the churches of Nerezi (1164), Milesevo (1235),
Sopocani (1265–1270), Gracanica (*c.* 1320), and elsewhere.

Important frescoes survive also in Bulgaria, for instance in
the churches of Boiana (1259) and St. George at Sofia (fourteenth
century), and at Kalotino (late fifteenth century), Dragalevici
(1476), and Arnabassi (1681). In Rumania, the finest wall paintings are in two churches at Curtea de Arges (fourteenth century).
In Russia, which was never part of the Byzantine Empire, except
for the Crimea, decoration by means of mural paintings was not so
extensively used. The most notable examples of frescoes in Russia
are in the cathedrals of St. Demetrios at Vladimir (1198) and of
the Transfiguration at Novgorod (1378).

The technique of the other major form of iconography, executed on panels, goes back to the Egyptian tomb paintings of the
Greco-Roman period. This technique is known as *tempera.* It employs an albuminous or colloidal medium, particularly egg, and
executes the icon on gesso-covered panels. As a rule, the gesso is
painted on a fine linen canvas that has been attached to a panel.

Few panel icons of the pre-iconoclastic period survive. Some of them date from as far back as the fifth or sixth century. Prior to the thirteenth century, single figures were usually depicted on panels. From the thirteenth century onwards, there is a noticeable increase in the number of icons depicting sacred events.

The art of panel iconography, like that of iconography in mosaic and fresco, was brought to Slavic countries by Greek artists of the Byzantine period. Thus, Theophanes the Greek (fourteenth and early fifteenth centuries) is well known both in connection with frescoes in Novgorod and Moscow, and for a number of panels that are preserved in the Tretiakov Gallery at Moscow. Russia's greatest iconographer, Andrew Rublev (c. 1370–c. 1430) was among Theophanes' pupils. Panel iconography flourished in Russia, unlike mural decoration, the development of which, as we have noted above, was somewhat restricted.[7]

Innumerable panel icons done in the Byzantine style are to be found in the older churches of the Orthodox countries. Such panels may also be seen in museums and private collections. The Byzantine Museum at Athens is devoted exclusively to the preservation of works of art of the Byzantine tradition, and has a very large collection of panel icons.

Orthodox art did not decline with the political and military decline of the Byzantine Empire, the beginning of which has been assigned by historians to the end of the twelfth century, and more particularly to the Fourth Crusade in 1204. In the fourteenth century, we find two remarkable schools of iconography, the Macedonian and the Cretan. These terms are largely conventional, as the styles did not originate in the regions denoted by them, and the works which bear their names are not confined to Macedonia and Crete. The names have, however, been very widely adopted, and now can hardly be dispensed with. Moreover, the choice of these names, as we shall see, is not without some justification.

The Macedonian School appears in the thirteenth century, but is rooted in Byzantine iconography of the preceding period. It differs from it in stressing the idealistic element, derived from Greek art. Its conception of form, landscape and color is Hellenistic. The forms it employs are broad, the colors light, with no sharp contrast

---

[7]   For iconography in Russia see Appendix C below.

between light and shade, the folds of the garments relatively simple. In the representation of the body, there is a tendency to approach nature, without ever faithfully copying it, but rather transforming it by injecting into it an element of idealism and by thoroughly spiritualizing it. This school grew up at Constantinople. It developed here and at Thessaloniki, second city of Byzantium. At Constantinople it tended towards greater idealism; at Thessaloniki, towards greater expressiveness. Thessaloniki served as the center of the school in that region. From this city the Macedonian School spread, through Greek artists, to Greek and Serbian Macedonia, and more generally in the Balkans. It reached Mystra early in the fourteenth century, probably directly from Constantinople. From the thirteenth century to the fourteenth, the Macedonian School was at its height. By the end of the fourteenth century it had lost its original vigor, and was becoming eclectic, borrowing elements from the folk tradition. After the fall of Constantinople to the Ottoman Turks (1453), the popular element became more and more prominent, until by the end of the sixteenth century the Macedonian school no longer existed.

Because of its characteristic breadth of conception, this style is more suited to the decoration of large surfaces than panels; and indeed little use was made of it in panel iconography. Few panels in which this style is used have survived. Mural decorations, on the other hand, are numerous. Examples are mosaics in the church of the Monastery of Chora (beginning of the fourteenth century), the frescoes in the side chapel of St. Euthymios in the Church of St. Demetrios at Thessaloniki (1303), the mosaics in the Church of the Holy Apostles at the same city (1312–1315), the frescoes in the Church of the Protaton at Karyes on Mount Athos (first quarter of the fourteenth century), those of the churches of St. Demetrios and Aphentiko or Brontocheiou at Mystra (*c.* 1310), and of Pantanassa, also at Mystra (1428), and those in the churches of Nagoricino (1316) and St. Nikitas (1309–1320) in Yugoslavia.

The greatest master of this school is Manuel Panselinos of Thessaloniki, who did the magnificent frescoes in the Church of the Protaton on the Holy Mountain of Athos.[8]

---

[8] See my books *Anchored in God,* pp. 33–42, 55, 68, and *Byzantine Thought and Art,* Belmont, Mass., 1968, 1974, pp. 79–84.

What has been termed the Cretan School is characterized by a closer attachment to the style of Byzantine painting prior to the thirteenth century. It employs tall and narrow forms, closely repeated folds of garments, darker colors, and sharp contrasts of light and shade. The place of origin of this school has not been definitely established. It was not Crete. In all probability it began, like the Macedonian School, at Constantinople and spread from there to Greece and elsewhere in the Balkans. Mystra soon became an important center of this school, which appears to have reached the city directly from Constantinople. Most probably it was from Mystra that it was transmitted to Crete, during the second half of the fourteenth century. From Crete the style spread to Meteora, Mount Athos, and other parts of Greece.

The Cretan School made its appearance in Constantinople early in the fourteenth century. It reached its highest point, both in wall and panel painting, in the sixteenth century, through Cretan iconographers on Mount Athos, who gave the style its definitive form. Theophanes the Cretan, who frescoed the main church and the refectory of the Monastery of Lavra on Mount Athos, is the greatest representative of this school. He gave the 'Cretan' fresco its classical form.

This school of iconography rivalled the Macedonian during the closing period of the Byzantine Empire. After the fall of Constantinople (1453), it became the dominant school of painting in the Orthodox Church.

Orthodox iconography remained faithful to the Byzantine tradition down to recent times. Russian iconographers began to break with this tradition in the seventeenth century; and the Westernizing reforms of Peter the Great brought about a disappearance of traditional iconography in Russia in the eighteenth century. In Greece, on the other hand, iconographers continued for the most part to paint in the Byzantine style until the early part of the nineteenth century. Following the Greek War of Independence (1821–1828), however, the strong influx of Western ideas into Greece, which resulted from the closer contact of Greece with Europe, led Greek iconographers to break with their tradition and adopt Western, particularly Italian, prototypes and techniques. The spirituality char-

acteristic of Byzantine painting was abandoned in favor of naturalism, and the tempera technique was replaced by the use of oil colors.
Typical of icon painters of this period is the attempt to 'correct' or
'improve' the austere, ascetic, unworldly forms of Byzantine iconography by means of perspective, faithfulness to anatomical detail,
and physical beauty. What happened in Russia and Greece, also
occurred in Rumania, Bulgaria, and Serbia. In Rumania, the break
with the Byzantine tradition of iconography took place at about the
same time as in Greece. The beginning was made by the first
Rumanian painters who were trained in Italy.

During the last decades, there has been a growing interest in
the older, Byzantine style iconography, in all of these countries, and
considerable activity directed towards the cleaning, preservation,
and safeguarding of works done in this style. In Greece there has
also been a significant revival of this style of iconography, thanks
especially to the initiative and efforts of the renowned icon painter
Photios Kontoglou (1895–1965). This revival has spread, through
the publication of his teachings[9] and the men whom he trained in
this art, to the United States and other countries. A similar revival
has been taking place in Rumania, effected by young painters who
have been using as their models icons in old Rumanian churches.
Among the Russians of the diaspora, too, there has been a significant
return to the traditional style of icon painting.

The revival of this style of iconography is bound to gain mo-
mentum from the increasing understanding and appreciation of
Byzantine art throughout the world.

---

[9] E.g., C. Cavarnos, *Byzantine Sacred Art: Selected Writings of the Contemporary Greek icon painter Fotis Kontoglous*, New York, 1957.

CHAPTER II

ICONOGRAPHIC DECORATION
OF CHURCHES

One of the most distinctive features of Eastern Orthodoxy is the extensive and systematic use of holy icons in churches. Every Orthodox church has an *iconostasis*, a wooden or marble screen supporting panel icons and separating the *bema* or sanctuary from the main body of the church, the nave. Also, there are *proskynetaria* or icon stands, on which special icons are placed for veneration. Except in very small chapels, there is at least one *proskynetarion*, with the icon of the sacred person or persons to whom the church is dedicated. The faithful cross themselves before this icon and kiss it upon entering the church. Panel icons are often attached to the walls. In addition to panels, an Orthodox church generally has a certain number of murals depicting sacred persons and incidents, executed either by brush or by inlaying small pieces of colored glass or stone, the latter being known as mosaics. Sculptured representations are rare, and are limited to bas-reliefs: statues are not employed. The reliefs themselves have the character of paintings.

In a typical Greek Orthodox church there are two tiers of icons on the iconostasis, a lower tier of large icons and an upper tier of considerably smaller ones. (In Russian churches the number of tiers has been increased to three.) The lower series always includes at least the following three icons: that of Christ, that of the Theotokos[1] and Child, and that of the sacred person, persons, or event specially celebrated by the particular church. The icon of Christ is invariably placed immediately to the south of the door which is at the middle of the iconostasis and is known as the

---

[1] 'The Godbirthgiver,' the All-Holy Virgin Mary, who gave birth to Christ God as man.

Beautiful Gate (*Horaia Pyle*), while that of the Theotokos is always placed immediately to the north of the Beautiful Gate. These icons are known as *Despotikai,* 'Sovereign.' The icon depicting the person or event specially celebrated by the church is customarily set next to that of the Theotokos, but sometimes beside that of Christ, particularly in small churches which have only three large icons on the iconostasis. In larger churches, the first row of icons almost always includes the icon of St. John the Forerunner and Baptist, placed immediately next to Christ's. Except in very small chapels, the lower tier comprises other icons, their number depending on the length of the iconostasis. The latter invariably has a side doorway on the north side, and in larger churches one on the south, too. When there are doors here, these are mounted with the icons of the archangels Michael and Gabriel — that of Michael is placed on the north door, that of Gabriel on the south. The tier of small icons on the upper part of the iconostasis comprises either representations of the 'Twelve Great Festivals' (the *Dodekaorton*), or of the twelve apostles, each festival or apostle being depicted separately. The 'Twelve Great Festivals' are the Annunciation, the Nativity, the Presentation of Christ in the Temple, the Baptism, the Transfiguration, the Raising of Lazarus, the Entrance into Jerusalem, the Crucifixion, the Resurrection, the Ascension, Pentecost, and the Dormition of the Theotokos.

Above the Beautiful Gate, at the top of the iconostasis, is placed a cross with the figure of Christ crucified. To the right of the crucifix stands the figure of the All-Holy Virgin, and to the left that of St. John the Theologian, depicted on panels. On the hinged doors (*bemothyra*), which form the lower part of the Beautiful Gate, there is usually a representation of the Annunciation.

The special importance given to the icons of the Virgin and the Baptist, in placing them on the iconostasis to the right and to the left of Christ, has its justification in statements made in the Gospels. The Virgin Mary is said to have "found favor with God," [2] to have been "overshadowed" by the power of the Highest,[3] to have miraculously conceived and given birth to the Son of God, Jesus

---

[2] Luke 1: 30.
[3] Luke 1: 35.

Christ;[4] while John the Baptist is characterized by Christ as "more than a prophet, for this is he of whom it is written, 'Behold I send my messenger before thy face, who shall prepare thy way before thee.' " [5]

In the decoration of a church with wall paintings or mosaics, certain areas are set apart for particular representations. Thus, the top part of the dome is used for the representation of Christ as *Pantocrator,* 'Ruler of All,' 'Almighty;' the spaces between the windows of the drum of the dome, for the prophets; the four pendentives below, for the evangelists; the vaults and upper walls in the nave, for the Twelve Great Festivals; the lower parts, for the miracles and parables of Christ; the lowest areas of all, for individual saints; the conch of the main eastern apse, for the Theotokos as *Platytera.* This is, in part, the general scheme that has prevailed in Orthodox churches during the last thousand years. The scheme varies somewhat from church to church, according to the shape and size of the building, the period when it was decorated, and the region where it is built. Thus, the scheme indicated above applies, so far as the dome is concerned, to the domed church; in a basilica there cannot very well be a central Pantocrator, and the prophets and evangelists have to be painted elsewhere. Also, in a small church, even when the representations are considerably reduced in scale, they must necessarily be fewer in number.

The domed church, rather than the domeless basilica, is typical of Eastern Orthodoxy, and expresses more successfully its distinctive spirit. In such a church, the figure of Christ as Pantocrator, depicted in the central dome, which dominates the whole edifice, is the largest and most impressive of all the icons. This representation consists of a large bust of Christ enclosed in a multicolored circle. The God-Man holds the book of the Gospels in His left hand and blesses with His right. His head, which is encircled with a large halo inscribed with a cross, His face, His neck and shoulders all suggest great power and magnificence. His facial expression is that of an all-seeing and austere, yet merciful, lawgiver and judge. This icon reminds the faithful of the words of the Apostle Paul: And

---

4   Luke 1: 32.
5   Matt. 11: 9–11.

God the Father "raised Him from the dead, and set Him at His own right hand in the heavenly places, far above all principality, and power, and might, and dominion, and every name that is named, not only in this world, but also in that which is to come; and hath put all things under His feet, and gave Him to be the head over all things to the Church, which is His body, the fulness of Him that filleth all in all." [6] It also reminds the faithful of the hymn: "Know and behold that I am God, Who searches the hearts and chastizes thoughts, scrutinizes acts, and sets sin on fire." [7]

It may be noted that the term 'Pantocrator' and the idea behind it appear in the book of Revelation. Thus, in 1: 8 it is said: "I am Alpha and Omega, saith the Lord Who is, and Who was, and Who is to come, the Pantocrator." Also, the use of the multicolored band around Him is based on Revelation 4: 3, where the *iris* or rainbow is said to surround the throne of God.

In churches where the size of the dome permits, the Pantocrator is often surrounded, on the round strip immediately below the iris, by the Theotokos, St. John the Forerunner, in an attitude of prayer, and angels. The Theotokos is painted on the east side of the strip; the Forerunner, on the west. Here is expressed in line and color what the closing part of the Divine Liturgy says in words: "May Christ our true God have mercy upon us, through the intercessions of His most pure and most blessed holy Mother; . . . and through the protection of the precious, incorporeal Spiritual Powers in heaven; through the supplications of the precious, glorious Prophet and Forerunner John the Baptist. . . ." The representation of the Theotokos so close to Christ Pantocrator and surrounded by a choir of angels is also in keeping with another part of the Liturgy, which says: "It is truly meet to bless thee, Theotokos, the ever-blessed and most pure Virgin and Mother of our God. Thee who art more honorable than the Cherubim and incomparably more glorious than the Seraphim, who, while chaste, didst bear God, the Logos; thee, who art verily the Theotokos, we magnify." The proximity of John the Baptist to Christ is justified by Christ's own characterization of the Baptist which has already been mentioned in connec-

---

[6] Ephesians 1: 20–23.
[7] *Triodion,* Venice, 1876, p. 261.

tion with his icon on the iconostasis. Sometimes he is depicted with
wings, according to this passage in Scripture: "Behold, I send my
messenger before thy face." [8] The word 'messenger' is a translation
of the Greek *angelos,* which means both messenger and angel.

Further down the dome, on the drum, are depicted Old Testament prophets: Moses, David, Solomon, Jeremiah, Habakkuk, Elijah, Isaiah, and others, with one or two between the windows.
Their number varies considerably, depending on the size of the
dome. The presence of the prophets here reminds the faithful who
turn their gaze upward to the dome of the troparion: "Thou hast
been seen by the prophets, O Master, as far as they had the capacity
of beholding Thy splendor; through their prayers, render us capable
of receiving Thy rays of illumination, having cleansed our souls of
sinful thoughts and feelings." [9]

Below the prophets, on the four pendentives (the spherical
triangles between the adjoining arches that support the dome) are
depicted the evangelists: Matthew, Mark, Luke, and John. Matthew
and John are always depicted in the northeast and southeast pendentives respectively, while Mark and Luke are usually painted in
the northwest and southwest. They are represented seated, engaged
in writing. John is depicted with his head turned back, according
to the statement in the book of Revelation: "I was in the Spirit on
the Lord's day, and heard behind me a great voice. . . . And I turned
to see the voice that spake with me." [10] Sometimes they are shown
with their symbols: Matthew, with an angel; Mark, with a lion;
Luke, with a calf; and John, with an eagle. This is in accordance
with the statement in the book of Revelation that round about the
throne of God "were four beasts full of eyes before and behind.
And the first beast was like a lion, and the second beast like a calf,
and the third beast had a face as a man, and the fourth beast was
like a flying eagle." [11]

Second in importance only to the central dome in mural decoration is the main eastern apse. The dominant figure here, that of

8   Matthew 10: 11.
9   *Parakletike,* Venice, 1851, p. 46.
10   1: 10, 12.
11   4: 6–7.

the All-Holy Virgin, appears in the conch or semidome. This icon is known as *Platytera.* The representation consists either of the upper half of her body, with arms outstretched in prayer, and the Child Christ against her chest, or of the entire figure, usually with the Child in her lap. In the latter case she is generally enthroned. The Child blesses with His right hand and holds a scroll in His left, or blesses with both hands. Often the Virgin is flanked on either side by the archangels Michael and Gabriel (to her right and left, respectively).

The representation of the Theotokos in this part of the church is in line with a very old tradition, and consonant with the Gospel assertion that Jesus Christ, Savior of mankind, was born of the the Virgin Mary; it also accords well with the architectural and hymnographic symbolism of the Eastern Church. Professor George A. Soteriou, the eminent Byzantinist, has this to say about the significance of depicting the Virgin here: "During the Byzantine period, the allegorical meaning of the apse as a point uniting the roof of the church with the floor, and symbolically heaven with the earth, contributed to the placing of the icon of the Theotokos as Platytera. The Theotokos hovers as it were between heaven and earth, as 'the heavenly Ladder, whereby God has descended,' and 'the Bridge leading those on the earth to heaven.' (The symbolism is taken from the Akathistos Hymn.) She is chiefly represented as praying before the Pantocrator in the dome, but also as holding the Child." [12]

The full name of this icon of the Virgin is 'She who is wider than the heavens' (*Platytera ton ouranon*). She is so called because she gave birth to Christ God, Who is the Creator of all things, present in them and transcendent of them. This appellation appears in various hymns to her, for example in the one which says: "When Gabriel said to thee, O Virgin, 'Rejoice,' with this utterance the Master of all became incarnate in thee, the holy Ark, as the righteous David said; thou wast shown to be wider than the heavens, having held thy Creator. . . ." [13]

On the area of the apse immediately below the Platytera is depicted the Divine Liturgy. In the middle of this composition

---

[12] *Nea Hestia,* Athens, 1955, Christmas issue, pp. 408–409.
[13] *Parakletike,* p. 42.

there is a ciborium with the Holy Table under it, on which rests
the Book of the Gospels. Christ, clad in episcopal vestments, and
assisted by angels who are dressed as deacons, officiates. Sometimes
the Divine Liturgy is depicted instead in the prothesis, the northern
apse of the sanctuary (*bema*), where the preparation of the sacred
elements of the Eucharist takes place during the first part of the
Liturgy.

Below the Divine Liturgy is represented the Holy Communion.
In the center there is a ciborium, with the Holy Table having a paten
and chalice on it, containing the Eucharistic bread and wine. Christ,
usually garbed in a tunic and mantle and assisted by two angels
dressed as deacons, offers the sacred elements to His disciples. This
composition bears the inscription: "Take, eat," [14] and "Drink ye
all, of it." [15]

On the lower part of the apse are depicted, in episcopal robes,
the great hierarchs: St. Basil the Great, St. Gregory Nazianzen, St.
Chrysostom, St. Athanasios the Great, and others, as space permits.
They are represented as taking part in the Liturgy.

The narthex, too, which runs across the west end of the church,
has traditionally been decorated with wall paintings or mosaics.
The most important area for iconographic decoration here is that
over the main entrance which leads to the nave. Usually a bust of
Christ as Teacher is painted here, the Lord blessing with His right
hand and holding in His left the book of the Gospels, open at the
statement: "I am the door: by me if any man enter in, he shall be
saved;" [16] or, "I am the light of the world: he that followeth me
shall not walk in darkness, but shall have the light of life." [17] On
either side of Him are the Theotokos and John the Forerunner,
turned towards Him in an attitude of prayer.

The other parts of the narthex — the vaults, walls, etc. — are
decorated with events from the life of the Theotokos and of the
martyrs, or with visions from Daniel and the book of Revelation,
as well as with individual saints, both full length figures and busts.

---

[14]   Matthew 26: 26.
[15]   Matthew 26: 27.
[16]   John 10: 9.
[17]   John 8: 12.

A definite pattern of church decoration was gradually developed, and this became more definitely established after the victory of the Church over Iconoclasm in 843. The system of arrangement is set forth in the *Explanation of the Art of Painting* (*Hermeneia tes Zographikes Technes*) by the Athonite monk Dionysios of Fourna (1670–*c.* 1745).[18] Although this work was first printed in the last century (1853), it was probably written about 1730, and is based on several anonymous earlier writings. In it, Dionysios explains how panel icons and frescoes are executed, how each saint or scene is to be depicted, and how the icons are to be arranged in domed churches and basilicas. Dionysios' book has been superseded by the *Explanation of Orthodox Iconography* (*Ekphrasis tes Orthodoxou Eikonographias*), written by Photios Kontoglou, the foremost modern Greek icon painter, and published in 1960 at Athens. Kontoglou's work is based on writings older than those which were employed by Dionysios of Fourna, as well as on his own extraordinarily rich experience as an iconographer and restorer of Byzantine paintings. It is free from certain errors and marks of Western influence that are to be found here and there in the book of Dionysios, and is written with greater clarity.

---

[18] This book is referred to by English writers as the *Painter's Guide*, or *Byzantine Guide to Painting*. It was translated in the last century into French by Paul Durand, and was published with an Introduction and numerous notes by Adolphe N. Didron under the title *Manuel d'iconographie chrétienne* in 1845 at Paris. The French version of Dionysios' work contained in Didron's *Manuel d'iconographie chrétienne* was translated into English by Margaret Stokes, and appears as Appendix II, "Byzantine Guide to Painting," in the English version of Didron's book, which was published, under the title *Christian Iconography; or, History of Christian Art in the Middle Ages,* in 1886 at London and was reprinted in 1965 at New York. Regarding Dionysios of Fourna, see my book *The Holy Mountain,* 1973, pp. 27–28.

CHAPTER III

THE FUNCTIONS OF ICONS

Holy icons serve a number of purposes. (1) They enhance the beauty of a church. (2) They instruct us in matters pertaining to the Christian faith. (3) They remind us of this faith. (4) They lift us up to the prototypes which they symbolize, to a higher level of thought and feeling. (5) They arouse us to imitate the virtues of the holy personages depicted on them. (6) They help to transform us, to sanctify us. (7) They serve as a means of worship and veneration. I shall discuss briefly each one of these functions.

(1) The most obvious function of icons is that they *enhance the beauty of a church.* Attention to this fact is called by the following hymn from the *Triodion* that is chanted on the eve of the Sunday of Orthodoxy, when the victory over Iconoclasm is commemorated:

> The Church of Christ is now embellished like a bride,
> having been adorned with icons of holy form; and
> it calls all together spiritually; let us come and cele-
> brate together joyfully with concord and faith, magni-
> fying the Lord.[1]

The idea that icons are a means of enhancing the beauty of churches appears in many writings of the Fathers. To give one example, Niketas Stethatos, the most famous disciple of St. Symeon the New Theologian (949–1022), says that upon becoming abbot of the Monastery of St. Mamas, Symeon "adorned its church with beautiful marbles on the pavement, with holy icons, and other wonderful offerings." [2]

It may be added, that the very fact that the Orthodox in

---

1 *Triodion,* Venice, 1876, p. 123.
2 *The Extant Works of Saint Symeon the New Theologian,* trans. by Dionysios Zagoraios, Syros, 1886, p. 6.

general speak of the 'decoration' (*diakosmesis*) of churches with icons shows plainly that they recognize this function.

As a 'house of God' and a 'house of prayer,' the church should be rendered as beautiful as possible, especially in the interior, where the faithful gather for worship. But the beauty of the church must bear the impress of holiness; and the pleasure evoked by it must transcend that of mere aesthetic experience: it must be spiritual.

(2) That icons serve *to instruct the faithful* is a point which is duly emphasized by the Greek Church Fathers. Thus, St. John Damascene remarks that since not every one is literate, nor has leisure for reading, the Fathers agreed that such things as the Incarnation of our Lord, His association with men, His miracles, His Crucifixion, His Resurrection, and so on, should be represented on icons.[3] And St. Photios, Patriarch of Constantinople, says: "Just as speech is transmitted by hearing, so a form through sight is imprinted upon the tablets of the soul, giving to those whose apprehension is not soiled by wicked doctrines a representation of knowledge consonant with piety." [4]

Photios adds that icons not only teach, as do written accounts, but in some instances they are *more vivid* than written accounts, and hence *superior* to the latter as a means of instruction. He cites as an example the representation of the deeds of holy martyrs.

We can also appreciate the effectiveness of icons as a means of instructing if we note that in a *composition,* such as the Nativity, the Raising of Lazarus, or the Crucifixion, the icon presents *simultaneously and concisely* many things — a place, persons and objects — that would take an appreciable period of time to describe in words.

(3) We have a tendency to forget, to forget even things that are of vital importance to us, to fall asleep spiritually. So even though we may *know* many things about the Christian faith, such as the commandment of love, the teaching about the spiritual realm, the exemplary character and noble deeds of many holy personages, we tend to *forget* them, as we become preoccupied with everyday

---

[3]   See the excerpt from St. John Damascene in Appendix A below.
[4]   Cyril Mango, *The Homilies of Photius,* p. 294. Cf. St. Basil: "What the spoken account presents through the sense of hearing, the painting silently shows by representations" (*P.G.,* Vol. 94, col. 1401a).

worldly matters and pursuits. Icons serve to *remind* us of these things, to *awaken* us with respect to them. The vivacity of icons, which St. Photios points out, renders icons very effective in this regard. John Damascene sums up this function when he calls them *concise memorials* (*hypomneseis*),[5] that is, concise means of remembering. He gives the following example: "Many times, doubtless, when we do not have in mind the Passion of our Lord, upon seeing the icon of Christ's Crucifixion, we recall His saving suffering."[6]

(4) Icons also serve *to lift us to the prototypes, to a higher level of consciousness, of thought and feeling.* This is their *anagogic* function. The prototypes of the icons, i.e. Christ, the Theotokos, the Prophets, Apostles, Martyrs, Saints in general, enjoy a higher level of being than we do in our ordinary, distracted everyday life. When we see their icons, we recall their superior character and deeds; and as we recall them, we think pure, sublime thoughts, and experience higher feelings. Thus, for a while we live on a higher plane of being. As St. John Damascene remarks, "we are led by perceptible icons to the contemplation of the divine and spiritual."[7]

In this function of the icon, its essentially symbolic nature is manifest. An icon is not an end in itself; it is not merely an aesthetic object to be enjoyed for whatever artistic merits it possesses, but is essentially a symbol, carrying us beyond itself. It is designed to lead us from the physical and psychophysical to the spiritual realm. And hence it is, as St. John Damascene says, a pattern (*typos*) of something heavenly.[8]

(5) By instructing us in the Christian religion, reminding us of its truths, aims and values, and lifting us up to the prototypes, to holy personages, icons serve another important purpose: *they stir us up to imitate the virtues of such personages.* Thus, one of decrees of the Seventh Ecumenical Synod — the Synod that was convoked specially to settle the dispute between the iconoclasts and those who defended the veneration of holy icons — says: "The more

---

5   Appendix A, below.
6   *Ibid.*
7   *P.G.*, Vol. 94, col. 1261a.
8   See Appendix A.

continually holy personages are seen in icons, the more are the beholders lifted up to the memory of the prototypes and to an aspiration after them." [9]

(6) An additional function served by holy icons is *to help transform our character, our whole being, to help sanctify us.* They effect this by instructing us, reminding us, uplifting us, and stirring us up morally and spiritually. The function of the icon in this regard is based on the principle that we become like that which we habitually contemplate. True icons focus the distracted, dispersed soul of man on spiritual perfection, on the divine. By dwelling steadily and lovingly on such perfection, we come to partake of it more and more.

(7) Finally, the icon has a *liturgical function, it is a means of worship and veneration.* This is one of its primary functions, more important than the first. Like sacred hymns and music, the icon is used as a means of worshipping God and venerating His saints. As such, it is *essentially symbolic,* leading the soul from the visible to the invisible, from the material to the spiritual, from the symbol to the prototype or original which it represents. As every Orthodox Christian knows, the first act of the faithful upon entering a church is to take a candle, light it and put it on a candlestand that is placed next to the *proskynetarion* or icon-stand on which is set the icon representing the sacred person, persons or event specially celebrated by the particular church and after whom or which it is named. Then he bows before the icon, making the sign of the cross, and kisses the icon, saying a brief prayer. This series of acts is called veneration or 'honorable reverence' of the icon. It is *not* an act of *worshipping* the icon. The Greek Church Fathers distinguish very sharply between 'honorable reverence' (*timetike proskynesis*), which is accorded to icons, and 'worship' (*latreia*). Worship is accorded only to God. Further, they emphasize that the veneration which we give to a holy icon goes to the prototype which it represents, for example, to Christ, to the Theotokos, to some martyr or other saint. In the words of Basil the Great, which have been repeated by John Damascene and other defenders of the icons, "the honor which is given to the icon passes over to the prototype" (*he time tes*

---

[9] *Ibid.*

eikonos eis to prototypon diabainei).[10] The prototype honored
is in the last analysis God, as God created man in His own image.[11]

   Neither God nor the saints, of course, need the honor which
we offer them, be it by means of icons, or by means of hymns and
music. But it is only proper for us to do so, as the adoration of God
and the admiration of saints are expressions of a soul that sees and
loves the beauty of holiness, of spiritual perfection, and feels grateful to the Deity and to holy men for their many benefactions to
mankind. Such a response is not merely something proper for us,
but is also conductive to our salvation. The following remark of
John Damascene calls attention to this point, and at the same time
has a bearing on several of the functions served by icons: "I enter
the common place-of-therapy of souls, the church, choked as it were
by the thorns of worldly thoughts. The bloom of painting attracts
me, it delights my sight like a meadow, and secretly evokes in my
soul the desire to glorify God. I behold the fortitude of the martyr,
the crowns awarded, and my zeal is aroused like fire; I fall down and
worship God through the martyr, and receive salvation." [12]

   When the various important functions of icons are ignored and
the crucial distinction between honorable reverence and worship is
lost sight of, iconoclasm, the condemnation of icons, is a result.
This is what happened in 726, when the Byzantine Emperor Leo
the Isaurian issued an edict which condemned the making and
veneration of icons as idolatry, and contrary to the second commandment. But the icon, as we have seen, is an image or symbol,
and is designed to lead us *to* that *of* which it is an image or symbol,
whereas an idol lacks this power of the authentic symbol; and the
veneration of an icon is *not* an act of 'worshipping' it. Hence the
charge of idolatry shows gross ignorance with regard to the nature
and functions of icons.

   In connection with the practice of according the reverence of
honor to holy icons, it should be remarked that this is deeply rooted
in the sacred tradition of Christianity. St. John Damascene would
trace the tradition of honorable reverence of sacred objects back to

---

10   *Ibid.*
11   St. Basil, *Concerning the Holy Spirit*, Ch. 18.
12   *P.G.*, Vol. 94, col. 1268 a–b.

the Mosaic people, who "venerated on all hands the *tabernacle* which was an image and type of heavenly things, or rather of the whole creation." [13] The *cross* has always been venerated by Christians. The painting of the cross in the dome or apse of the Church was not forbidden in Byzantium even by the fanatical enemies of the icons, the Iconoclasts. Now the crucifix is itself an icon, an image of Christ's crucifixion, a symbol of Christ Himself, Who is usually depicted upon it in the Eastern Orthodox Church.

---

[13]   See Appendix A.

Chapter IV

THEOLOGY AND AESTHETICS
OF BYZANTINE ICONOGRAPHY

The Greek Fathers, who formulated the dogmas of the Orthodox Church, did not specify just how icons should be painted. They did convey, however, the basic idea of true iconography, which is that everything in the icon should be reminiscent of a realm different from the material world, and of men who have been regenerated into eternity.[1] Thus the idea of a spiritual realm and transfigured men is the key to painting and understanding true icons.[2] The archetypes of the recurring themes of Byzantime iconography, such as those of Christ the Pantocrator, the Nativity, the All-Holy Virgin and the Child Christ, and St. John the Baptist, developed slowly. They are the result of centuries of spiritual life, Christian experience, genius and work. The painters who developed them regarded their work as fearful, like the dogmas of the true Faith; and they worked with humility and piety on the models that had been handed down to them by earlier iconographers, avoiding all inopportune and inappropriate changes. Through long elaboration, the various representations were freed from everything superfluous and inconstant, and attained the greatest, most perfect expression and power.[3]

Having a religious theme, such as Christ, or the Apostle Paul, does not suffice to make a painting an icon, an object suitable for liturgical use. *Its mode of expression must be spiritual,* that is, such as to make it *anagogic,* pointing to a reality beyond the physical,

---

[1] See Appendix A.

[2] Cf. Leonide Ouspensky, *L'Icone, vision du monde spirituel: quelques mots sur son sens dogmatique,* Paris, 1948, pp. 10–11.

[3] Cf. Photios Kontoglou, *Ta Akelidota Archetypa* ("The Spotless Archetypes"), *Nea Hestia,* Vol. 33, No. 385 (June, 1943), p. 780.

lifting those who see it to a higher level of thought, feeling and consciousness, denoted by the term spiritual.

This anagogic mode of expression is achieved in part by the use of a type of distortion. Thus, the proportions of a figure are distorted, some parts being exaggerated and others diminished.[4] The head, for instance, may be depicted disproportionately large, in order that the face, which is the most expressive part of the body, may be seen more distinctly. Usually, the eyes are depicted larger than they normally are, in order to express more effectively certain qualities which are thought of as spiritual.[5] Also, the nose is made rather thin, the mouth small, the fingers thin and elongated, in order to present an external expression of the transfigured state of the saint, whose senses have been refined, spiritualized.[6] The body is often elongated, as a further means of 'dematerialization.' Mountains, trees, buildings and so on are schematic, abstract. Thus, a mountain is represented by stair-like rock; a tree, by a trunk with a few branches; a city, by a few simple buildings surrounded by a fortification wall. Further dematerialization is attained by reducing space to a minimum, and by suppressing perspective and physical light.[7] Thus the figures depicted give the impression of being two-dimensional, like visions.[8] Finally, the iconographer makes no attempt to imitate faithfully the colors of nature, but uses extensively non-natural, mystical colors.

The anagogic element is present in all authentic icons, even in those in which the theme would seem to preclude this — for instance, the Crucifixion. In Byzantine iconography, which is Christian iconography par excellence, the Crucifixion is not a gruesome spectacle as it often is in Western paintings of the modern period.

---

[4] Cf. P. A. Michelis, *An Aesthetic Approach to Byzantine Art*, London, 1955, pp. 118, 197.

[5] That such qualities are expressed through the body is emphatically asserted by Byzantine theologians. Thus, St. John Climacos says: "When the whole man is in a manner commingled with the love of God, then even his outward appearance in the body, as in a kind of mirror, shows the splendor of his soul" (St. John Climacos, *The Ladder of Divine Ascent*, trans. by Lazarus Moore, New York *c.* 1960, p. 264).

[6] Cf. Leonide Ouspensky and Vladimir Lossky, *The Meaning of Icons*, Boston, 1955, p. 39.

[7] Cf. André Grabar, *Byzantine Painting*, Geneva, 1953, p. 39.

[8] Cf. P. A. Michelis, *op. cit.*, pp. 116–117, 157.

Christ's body is not represented as the dead body of an ordinary, unregenerate man, far less as a corpse in a state of decomposition — as in the Crucifixion by Mathias Grunewald — inspiring horror and revulsion. Everything in the Byzantine depiction of the Crucifixion gives intimations of immortal life. The body depicted is that of the God-Man, and hence incorruptible. The expression of His face and body is full of heavenly calm and grandeur. There is an expression of sorrow in His face, but this sorrow is pervaded by gentleness and forgiveness. And he who contemplates the figure of Christ thus represented feels sorrow, though not the sorrow of despair, but the sorrow that contains the consoling hope in the triumph over death, in the Resurrection. If one turns one's gaze from the figure of Christ to the Theotokos and John the disciple, who stand on either side of the Cross, one observes an expression not of hysterical grief and horror, but of restrained, calm sorrow that is sweetened by the hope in immortality.[9]

The figures and objects depicted in a genuine icon may appear to some as simply unnatural; but they effectively express what photographic likenesses of nature cannot — higher states and qualities, and the essential nature of things. Renaissance paintings lack this anagogic element which true icons have; they give the illusion of materiality. The paintings of the Renaissance artists, such as da Vinci and Raphael, express physical rather than spiritual beauty. These works, which observe carefully the anatomical details of the body and use perspective in a mathematical way, and colors and forms that we are accustomed to see in the world about us, in order to give the illusion of material reality, are ruled out as icons. True iconography is intended to take us beyond anatomy and the three-dimensional world of matter to a realm that is immaterial, spaceless, timeless — the realm of the spirit, of eternity. And hence the forms and colors are not those that one customarily observes around him, but have something unworldly about them. The iconographer does not endeavor to give the illusion of material reality, a photographic likeness of men, mountains, trees, animals, buildings, and so on. He

---

9   See Photios Kontoglou, *He Apelpisia tou Thanatou eis ten Threskeutiken Zographiken tes Dyseos, kai he Eirenochytos kai Pleres Elpidos Orthodoxos Eikonographia* ("The Despair of Death in Religious Paintings of the West, and Peace-pervaded and Full of Hope Orthodox Iconography"), Athens, 1961.

gives a schematic representation of these, leaving out everything that is not essential. He retains details only if they are necessary.

If religious works such as those of the Renaissance painters cannot be called icons, much less can sentimental, arbitrary products of the imagination, simply because they happen to have a religious subject, and still less should one give the name of 'icon' to the creations of certain artists who, seeking to be 'original' at any cost and thoroughly 'modern,' wantonly distort and dehumanize the forms of sacred personages. The departures from anatomical accuracy and naturalness in general seen in icons of the Byzantine tradition have led some to see a certain affinity between Byzantine iconography and recent schools of painting. But Byzantine painting and these schools are quite unrelated in the *use* which they make of the distortion of the human figure. These recent trends, known as 'cubism,' 'expressionism,' 'abstract art' and so on, when they are anything more than experiments in technique, seem to be attempts to express by means of dislocated heads, occluded eyes, monstrous breasts, and the like, the disintegrated state of contemporary man,[10] rather than to represent contemporary man's yearning for a higher reality, beyond the material, and an aspiration to be in relation with such a reality. What one finds in these works is a complete negation of the divine image in man; what one misses in them is not only a trace of external, physical beauty, but also any suggestion of inner, spiritual beauty. As I pointed out earlier, an icon is *essentially a symbol,* and a symbol which is designed to lead one from the physical and psychophysical realms to the spiritual realm.

True iconography is opposed to the ideas that art should copy nature, or should express the imagination or personality of the artist, or the spirit of his time. It aims to give the most effective expression to the universal truths and values of Christian religion; to lift the contemplator to the apprehension and experience of them; to transform and sanctify him. To this end the icon painter adheres faithfully to the classical Christian tradition of sacred painting, the Byzantine, employing its consecrated archetypes and techniques,

---

[10] On the significance of such forms in Picasso's paintings, cf. Herbert Read, *The Philosophy of Modern Art,* Cleveland, 1962, p. 176.

avoiding arbitrariness and improvisation, as well as all that is vague,
superfluous, subjective, sensual — in general, everything which
tends to keep the contemplator of works of art chained to a lower
level of being. The art of authentic iconography is *eminently de-
liberate, clear, precise, simple, objective, universal, spiritual.*

A true icon expresses *spiritual beauty.* The notion of spiritual
beauty appears in philosophical and theological writings of Antiquity, the Medieval Period, and the Modern Age. Plato says much
about it in discussing the Idea of the Good in the *Republic* and Ab-
solute Beauty in the *Symposium,* and in treating of justice, self-
mastery, and the other virtues of the soul. Plotinos speaks of it in
the *Enneads,* when he deals with Beauty, the Intelligence, and the
virtues. St. Augustine refers to God in his *Confessions* as "the most
Beautiful of all." [11] Descartes, the father of modern European
philosophy, speaks of 'the incomparable beauty of the inexhaustible
light," [12] meaning God. Leibniz speaks of "the beauties of souls
which never perish and never cause displeasure."[13] And Alfred
North Whitehead tells us that "the contemplation of the beauty of
holiness" belongs to the essence of religion.[14] Such passages testify
to the persistent recognition that the category of the beautiful ex-
tends beyond the physical realm to the spiritual. This recognition
is most marked in Byzantine theological writings, which provide
the doctrinal foundations of Byzantine iconography. The notion of
spiritual beauty recurs frequently in the writings of such eminent
representatives of this theology as Sts. Basil the Great, John
Chrysostom, Gregory of Nyssa, Maximos the Confessor, John Damascene, and Symeon the New Theologian. They often view man's
striving for spiritual perfection and union with God as a striving
for the attainment of beauty of the soul and the vision of the
beauty of God. For they view God as the supremely beautiful
Being, and the virtues of the soul as rendering her a likeness of
God, hence beautiful; and likeness to God as leading to the vision
of God, to union with Him. Thus, St. Gregory of Nyssa says: "This

---

[11] II. 6.
[12] *Meditations,* III.
[13] Leibniz, *Philosophical Writings,* London, 1934, p. 256.
[14] *Science and the Modern World,* New York, 1925, p. 165.

union of the soul with the incorruptible Deity can be accomplished in no other way but by herself attaining by her virgin state to the utmost purity possible, — a state which, being like God, will enable her to grasp that to which it is like, while she places herself like a mirror beneath the purity of God, and moulds her own beauty at the touch and the sight of the Archetype of all beauty." [15] Not only in the writings of the Greek Church Fathers, but also in the compositions of Byzantine hymnographers, there is a frequent dwelling on the beauty of God and the aspiration for beauty of the soul. The following hymn is an example:

> Make straight the hearts of Thy servants
> towards the unapproachable light, O Thrice
> resplendent Lord, and bestow the effulgence
> of Thy glory upon our souls, that we may
> behold Thine ineffable beauty.[16]

The word 'spiritual' as used here is based on the distinction of reality into higher and lower levels, as in the Divided Line of Plato.[17] Spiritual reality is the highest level. To it belong God and man's highest psychical activities and qualities. There are gradations within this level: God is superior to His creatures. Intuitive reason, conscience, qualities such as meekness, humility, and love of God and neighbor belong to the level of spiritual reality. Discursive reason and its objects represent a lower level, while the senses, the imagination and their objects, as well as ordinary, mundane desires and feelings, such as anger, malice, jealousy, bodily pleasure and pain, and the like, represent a still lower level.

In terms of *beauty,* a true icon is one that expresses spiritual beauty, rather than physical beauty. By spiritual beauty is meant the beauty of holiness. God is holy; [18] and man becomes holy by attaining likeness to God through the acquisition of all the virtues. A full treatment of this subject would require a book. I shall limit myself, therefore, to a brief explanation of those virtues which the

---

[15] *A Select Library of Nicene and Post-Nicene Fathers,* Second Series, Vol. V, p. 356.

[16] *Parakletike,* Venice, 1851, p. 94.

[17] *Republic* VI, 509d–511e.

[18] Leviticus 11: 44, 19: 2, 20: 7, 1 Peter 1: 15–16, etc.

Church Fathers of Byzantium especially stress, basing myself on
their teaching, and will say something about the manner in which
they are expressed in Byzantine iconography. Specifically, I shall
discuss the virtues of faith, meekness, humility, freedom from passions, and love.

Faith is of two kinds: that which is based on hearing, and that
which is based on inner perception. The first kind of faith consists
in the free acceptance of the true dogmas concerning God and His
creatures, both intelligible and sensible. It is possessed by all the
Orthodox. The second kind of faith is possessed only by those who
have been illumined by Divine grace. It is called 'substantial'
(*hypostatike*) faith.[19] When the author of the Epistle to the Hebrews defines faith as "the substance of things hoped for, the evi-
dence of things not seen," [20] he is speaking of the second, higher
order of faith. So is St. Maximos the Confessor (580–662), when
he says: "Faith is knowledge that has undemonstrable principles,
and hence is a relation that transcends nature." [21] The second kind
of faith grows out of the first; it does not contradict, but confirms
the first. Both orders of faith lift their possessors above the knowledge given by the physical senses and discursive reason; but the
second is knowledge and not, like the first, mere belief. He who has
risen to the second faith *knows*, in part. the transcendent realm of
mysteries; for he has seen, even though darkly, as "through a
·glass." [22] The circular, golden or ochre, halo around the head is
the most striking means which the iconographer employs in order to
symbolize the second type of faith. The halo is symbolic of the state
of illumination, of higher knowledge, as well as of victory over
death and of sanctity in general. Those who have only risen to the
first order of faith are represented without the halo, but are dis-
tinguished from unbelievers by the trust and reverence which they
show towards Christ and other sacred persons, expressed by their
gaze, posture and gestures.

---

[19]   See e.g. *Philokalia*, 4th ed., Athens, 1957–1963, Vol. 4, p. 335. All
other references to the *Philokalia* will be to this edition.

[20]   Hebrews 11: 1.

[21]   *Philokalia*, Vol. 2, p. 111.

[22]   1 Cor. 13: 9–12; *Philokalia*, Vol. 4, p. 335.

Out of faith grow *meekness* and the other virtues. Meekness is a habit of the soul that is characterized by freedom from anger and other forms of inner agitation, and is manifested in relation to all other men as steadfast gentleness. It remains unaffected by both insults and praises. The theologians of Byzantium extol this virtue, reminding us that the great Moses was meek above all other men; and that Jesus enjoins us to become imitators of His meekness. St. Mark the Ascetic (fl. 430) remarks: "He who is meek according to God is wiser than the wise;" and: "One's knowledge (of higher reality) is true to the extent that it is confirmed by meekness, humility, and love." [23] And St. Nilos (fl. 442) says that prayer — which is the highest form of inner activity, being a converse and union with God — "grows out of meekness and freedom from anger." [24] Iconography expresses this virtue by depicting the faces and gestures of the sacred personages free from all agitation, calm. Even when they are represented in situations that we associate with inevitable anger and excitement, the saints have an expression of angerlessness and serenity. One notes this, for instance, in the depiction of St. George killing the dragon, St. Demetrios in piercing Lyaeus, and the holy martyrs in the midst of all the tortures to which they are subjected.

Closely related to meekness is *humility*. St. John Climacos asserts that meekness is a precondition of humility: "The morning light precedes the sun, and the precursor of all humility is meekness." [25] Humility should not be confused with servility, which has nothing beautiful about it, being a form of cowardice. True humility is self-knowledge. A man is humble if he sees himself as he actually is and in relation to what he can and ought to become. One is humble if he is keenly aware of his shortcomings, of how far he falls short of Divine perfection. Humility in man is precisely this awareness become habitual and occasioning, on the one hand, a strong dissatisfaction with oneself, and on the other, a longing to rise towards the infinite perfection of God, according to Christ's precept: "Be ye perfect, as your Father Who is in heaven is per-

---

23   *Philokalia,* Vol. 1, p. 115.

24   *Ibid.,* p. 178.

25   *The Ladder of Divine Ascent,* p. 186.

fect." [26] Thus, humility is a mode of self-transcendence, like faith and meekness; it is a rising above the natural to the Divine realm. Contained in true humility is a feeling of one's insufficiency, of one's unworthiness, of the need of Divine help and mercy in order to effect the ascent. Like the virtues of faith and meekness, humility is indicated in the icon by the facial expression, posture and gestures of the sacred person depicted. It is especially symbolized by the bowed head and body. Occasionally it is symbolized more strikingly by depicting the saint kneeling, as in the well-known mosaic in the Church of the Holy Wisdom (*Hagia Sophia*) at Constantinople that shows the Byzantine Emperor Leo VI the Philosopher kneeling at the feet of Christ, receiving from Him the investiture of holy wisdom.

Humility prepares one for the development and manifestation of *passionlessness* or *dispassion* (*apatheia*). This virtue consists in freedom from all passions. The term 'passions' (*pathe*) in the Greek Patristic writings means not only such feelings as anger, greed and lust, but also all vice, overt sin, and all bad or negative thoughts. Passionlessness is a result of a long and sustained process of purification effected by a life in accordance with the Divine commandments. Thus, it is identical with purity (*katharotes*); and the Byzantines use the two terms interchangeably. In the order of acquisition, it comes *after* the virtues that have been mentioned — faith, meekness, humility — and others. In the *Ladder of Divine Ascent,* which embraces 30 steps leading to spiritual perfection, this virtue constitutes the 29th step; after it comes love, the highest of the virtues. It is because passionlessness is a result of a multitude of virtues that John Climacos remarks: 'The firmament has the stars for its beauty, and dispassion has the virtues for its adornment." [27] The iconographer succeeds in expressing this virtue by avoiding everything in his sacred figures that suggests pettiness or moral weakness, and by enduing them with an air of solemnity, hieraticalness, and spiritual grandeur. The sacred personages usually look directly at the beholder with serene faces and wide open eyes that seek to hide nothing, but express great inner strength and complete self-mastery.

---

[26]   Matthew 5: 48.

An accompaniment of freedom from passions is the manifestation of *spiritual love,* which is "the last of the virtues in the order of acquisition, but the first in the order of value," [28] being "the fullness of the law of perfection according to Christ." [29] Love manifests itself at different levels: there is sensuous love — love of physical beauty, bodily pleasure, and of material things in general; psychical love — love of honor, fame, power; and spiritual love — love of God, in the first place, and of man as an image of God, in the second. More than any other virtue, spiritual love renders man a likeness of God and unites him with the Deity. The Greek Fathers often quote the statement of the Gospel-writer John that "God is love, and he that dwelleth in love dwelleth in God, and God in him." [30] Love of God is love of Him as the supreme, all-beautiful, all-good, all-perfect personal Being and the aspiration for union with Him by grace. This union is called *theosis,* 'deification,' and is the final end for which man was created. The expression of this virtue in an icon is not effected by giving the figures a sugary facial expression or theatrical gestures. In an icon everything, including the expression of love, is characterized by solemnity, which arises from the feeling of awe towards God or reverence for God's image, man. One notes this even when two saints, such as the apostles Paul and Peter, embrace each other. When the object of love is Christ, the saint who gazes at the God-Man has the expression and gestures appropriate to worship.

Through the acquisition of all the virtues man becomes, as far as possible, a likeness of God, reflecting in his character and life the Archetypal beauty of the Deity. The acquisition of the virtues, of spiritual beauty, is not a matter of putting into the soul something totally absent from it, but of *developing* and *manifesting* the beauty already present in it, though in a potential and hidden state. According to the book of Genesis, God created man in His own image and likeness.[31] For the Byzantines this is not an empty formula, but

---

27 P. 258.
28 *Philokalia,* Vol. 1, p. 111.
29 *Ibid.,* p. 240.
30 1 John 4: 16.
31 1: 26.

a truth full of important implications for man. Thus, Gregory of Nyssa says: "God's perfect goodness is seen by His both bringing man into being from nothing, and fully supplying him with all gifts. But since the list of individual good gifts is a long one, it is out of the question to apprehend it numerically. The language of Scripture therefore expresses it concisely by a comprehensive phrase, in saying that man was made 'in the image of God.' For this is the same as to say that He made human nature participant in all good; for if the Deity is the fullness of good, and this is His image, then the image finds its resemblance to the Archetype in being filled with all good. Thus there is in us the principle of all excellence, all virtue and wisdom and every higher thing that we conceive." [32] Similarly, Abba Dorotheos (end of the 6th and beginning of the 7th centuries) remarks: "When God created man, He sowed in him the virtues; for He says: "Let us make man in our image and likeness." [33] Ancestral sin, the Fall, did not result in the destruction of the divine image in man, of the reflection of the Archetypal beauty in the soul, but only in its suppression, its concealment in subconsciousness. Dorotheos stresses that "the seeds of virtue are never destroyed." [34] When the suppressing factors — the passions, sin — are removed, the latent virtues are manifested again. Touching on this point, Athanasios the Great says: "When the soul gets rid of all the filth of sin which covers it and retains only the likeness of the image in its purity, then surely this latter being thoroughly brightened, the soul beholds as in a mirror the Image of the Father, even the Word (*Logos*), and by His means reaches the idea of the Father, Whose Image the Savior is." [35] In the same vein, Gregory of Nyssa writes: When sin entered, "that godly beauty of the soul which was an imitation of the Archetypal Beauty, like fine steel blackened with the vicious rust, preserved no longer the glory of its familiar essence, but was disfigured with the ugliness of sin." [36]

[32] *A Select Library of Nicene and Post-Nicene Fathers,* Second Series, Vol. V, p. 405.

[33] *P.G.,* Vol. 88, col. 1757.

[34] *Ibid.,* col. 1745.

[35] *A Select Library of Nicene and Post-Nicene Fathers,* Second Series, Vol. IV, p. 22.

[36] *Ibid.,* Vol. V, p. 357.

When "the earthly envelopment (of sin) is removed, the soul's beauty will again appear." [37]   Hence we should exert ourselves "to clear away the filth of sin, and so cause the buried beauty of the soul to shine forth again." [38]

Now inasmuch as icons teach us, remind us, lift us up to the prototypes, and arouse us to emulate the sacred persons and deeds depicted, they help us 'brighten' the divine image within us, they aid us in uncovering and developing the beauty of holiness. In other words, they help man attain likeness to God.

Moreover, inasmuch as likeness to God is the final stage of spiritual development preceding *theosis,* icons aid us in achieving *theosis,* 'deification.' *Theosis* is union with God through grace, a participation in the perfection of God, in the Divine Life. That 'likeness to God' is a necessary condition for union with Him is frequently asserted by the Eastern Church Fathers. Thus, Antony the Great says: "Through likeness to God we become united with God; through unlikeness we are separated from God." [39] And Kallistos Kataphygiotis (probably 12th century) remarks: "The supreme object of our aspiration is the supra-rational union of the soul with God; for this divine union, likeness to God is necessary." [40] The everlasting abiding in *theosis* is called salvation (*soteria*). In the words of Symeon the New Theologian, the greatest of the Byzantine mystics and a strong believer in the value of icons for man's spiritual ascent, "salvation is deliverance from all evils and the eternal finding in God of all blessings." [41]

The efficacy of the authentic icon in this regard has as its basis the principle that "we become like that which we habitually contemplate." True icons focus the distracted, dispersed soul of man on the Divine and arouse in him the desire to emulate those who have achieved spiritual beauty. Byzantine iconography, which seeks to give symbolic expression to this beauty, is based on the proper respect for the great power which the impact of a man who is what

---

[37] *Ibid.,* p. 358.
[38] *Ibid.*
[39] *Philokalia,* Vol. 1, p. 24.
[40] *Ibid.,* Vol. 5, p. 12.
[41] *The Extant Works of Saint Symeon the New Theologian,* 1886, Part II, p. 24.

he ought to be has for the inner transformation of those who have not advanced to this stage. It seeks to help solve the problem of human regeneration by inciting the beholder to see more clearly and more steadily Him Whom to see is to love, and loving Whom one becomes what He originally intended us to be.

1. Proskynetarion, adorned with mosaic designs made of mother-of-pearl. 1779. Nave of the Church of the Transfiguration at Megalochorion, Lesbos. At the left, a candle stand.

2. Iconostasis. Chapel of the Three Great Hierarchs, Monastery of Barlaam, Meteora.

3. The Theotokos as *Platytera.* Ca. 1950. Fresco by Photios Kontoglou, Church of Kapnikarea, Athens.

4. The Theotokos as *Hodegetria* (Guide) and the Child Christ. XIIth century. Mosaic, Monastery of St. Catherine, Mount Sinai.

5. The Theotokos as *Glykophilousa* (the Sweetly Kissing Mother).
1955. Large panel icon for iconostasis, by Photios Kontoglou. Private
collection of Constantine Cavarnos.

6. Christ the Pantocrator. XIVth century. Panel icon in the
Church of St. Therapon, Mytilene.

7.   Christ the Merciful.   1952.   Panel icon by Photios
Kontoglou.   Iconostasis of the Church of St. Euthymios,
Piraeus.

8. St. John the Baptist. XVIth century. Panel icon, Church of the Protaton, Mount Athos.

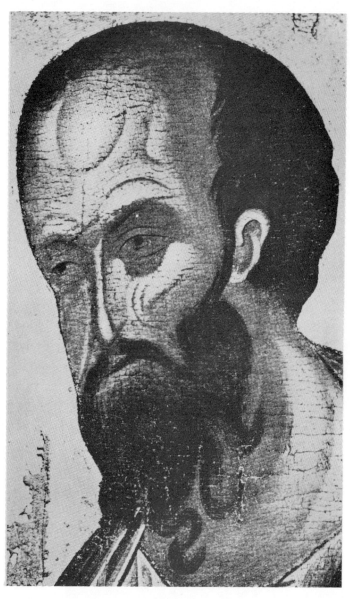

9. St. Paul the Apostle. Detail. Early XVth century. Panel
icon by Andrew Rublev.

10. Christ the Pantocrator. *Ca.* 1100. Mosaic in the dome, Church of Daphni, near Athens.

11. Fully decorated dome. 1957. Frescoes by Photios Kontoglou and his pupils, Church of St. Nicholas at Kato Patesia, Athens.

О ΠΡΟΦΗΤΗΣ

ΙΕΡΕΜΙΑΣ

ΟΥΤΟС
ΟΘΕΟС
ΗΜΩΝ
ΟΥΛΟΓΙ
СΘΗСΕ
ΤΑΙΕΤΕ
ΡΟСΓΡΟС
ΑΥΤΟΝ

12. The Prophet Jeremiah.   1972.   Mosaic by Demetrios Dukas,
Church of the Holy Wisdom (*Hagia Sophia*) at Washington, D.C.

13. St. Luke the Evangelist. Detail. 1971. Mosaic by **Demetrios**
Dukas in the southwest pendentive, Church of the Holy Wisdom at
Washington, D.C.

14. **The Nativity.** 1462. Wall painting, Church of the Holy Cross at Agiasmati, Cyprus.

15.   The Baptism of Christ.   Xth century.   Miniature in a manuscript,
Monastery of Iviron, Mount Athos.

16. The Crucifixion. XIth century. Mosaic, Church of the Monastery of Hosios Lukas, Boeotia.

17. The Resurrection. XIth century. Mosaic, Church of the Monastery of Hosios Lukas.

18. The Ascension. *Ca.* 1950. Fresco by Photios Kontoglou, Church of Zoodochos Pighi at Liopesi, Attica.

19. Group of Martyrs in prayer. XIVth century. Fresco, Church of Aphentiko, Mystra.

20. St. George the Great Martyr. Probably XVIIth century.
Panel icon, Church of St. Symeon, Mytilene.

21. The Prophet Zacharias. XIVth century. Detail. Fresco by
Manuel Panselinos, Church of the Protaton, Mount Athos, as copied
in 1955 by Spyros Papanikolaou, a pupil and assistant of Kontoglou.

22. St. Symeon Nemanya. 1314. Fresco, Church of Studenitza, Yugoslavia.

23. Three Angels. Depiction known as the Holy Trinity. *Ca.* 1411.
Panel icon by Andrew Rublev, Tretiakov Gallery, Moscow.

24. Sts. Euthymios and Savvas. 1535. Fresco by Theophanes the Cretan, main church of the Monastery of Lavra, Mount Athos.

APPENDIX A

TWO AUTHORITATIVE
EARLY CHRISTIAN TEXTS

1. St. John Damascene:

Concerning the Holy Icons[1]

Since some find fault with us for venerating (*proskynousi*) and honoring (*timosi*) the icon (*eikon*) of our Savior and of our Lady, and also the icons of the rest of the saints and servants of Christ, let them hear that in the beginning God created man according to His own image (*eikon*).[2] On what grounds, then, do we show reverence to each other, except that we have been made according to God's image? For as that great expounder of divine things, Basil, says, *"the honor which is given to the icon passes over to the prototype (prototypon)."* Now a prototype is that which is imaged (*eikonizomenon*), is that from which the derivative is obtained.

On what grounds did the Mosaic people honor, from all around, the *tabernacle*,[3] which bore an *image (eikon)* and *pattern (typos)* of heavenly things, or rather of the whole creation? Indeed, God said to Moses: "See, thou shalt *make them according to the pattern* which was shown thee in the mount."[4] And the *Cherubim, which overshadowed the mercy seat,* are they not the

---

[1] Excerpt from *An Exact Exposition of the Orthodox Faith,* Book IV, Chapter 16. I have made the translation from the ancient Greek text contained in Migne's *Patrologia Graeca,* 1864, Vol. 94, cols. 1168–1176. In this text, and in the excerpts from the decrees of the Seventh Ecumenical Synod that follow, I have italicized certain words, phrases, and sentences which seem to me to be especially important for understanding the ideas which these texts seek to convey.

[2] Genesis 1: 26.

[3] Exodus 33: 10.

[4] *Ibid.,* 25: 40; Hebrews 8: 5.

work of men's hands?[5] What, moreover, is the far-famed *temple at Jerusalem?* Is it not *hand-made,* and built by the *art of men?*[6]

Furthermore, Holy Scripture speaks against those who worship sculptured images (*glypta*), and also those who sacrificed to demons (*daimonia*). The Gentiles sacrificed, and the Judeans also sacrificed; but the Gentiles to demons and the Judeans to God. And the sacrifice of the Gentiles was rejected and condemned, but that of the righteous was very acceptable to God. For Noah sacrificed, and "God smelled the sweet scent" [7] of good-choice, and accepted the fragrance of good-will towards Him. Thus, the sculptured images of the Gentiles, since they were representations of demons, were rejected and forbidden.

But besides this, who can make an imitation of the invisible, incorporeal, uncircumscribed, and formless God? To give, therefore, form to the Deity (*to Theion*) is the height of madness and impiety.[8] Hence, in the Old Testament the use of icons was not common. But after God in His deep compassion became in truth man[9] for our salvation, not as He was seen by Abraham[10] in the form of man, nor as He was seen by the Prophets, but truly in essence man, and after He lived upon the earth and associated with men, worked miracles, suffered, was crucified, rose again and was taken back to Heaven, since all these things did in fact take place and were seen by men, they were written for the remembrance of us who were not living at that time, in order that though we did not see, we may, by hearing and believing, obtain the blessing of the Lord. *But since not every one is literate, nor has leisure for reading, the Fathers agreed that these things should be represented on icons,* as being acts of supreme heroism (*aristeia*), *in order that they should serve as a concise memorial* (*hypomnesis syntomos*) of them.[11]

---

5   Exodus 25: 18.

6   III Kings, Ch. 8 (Septuagint).

7   Genesis 8: 21.

8   John Damascene rules out here the possibility of making icons depicting the divine *essence.*

9   John 1: 14.

10   See e.g. Genesis 18: 1–8.

11   This, and the fact of Christ's Incarnation, referred to in the preceding sentence, provide a firm basis for representing Christ on icons.

Many times, doubtless, when we do not have in mind the Passion of our Lord, *upon seeing the icon* of Christ's Crucifixion, we *recall* His saving suffering and fall down and worship, *not the material, but that which is represented* — just as we do not venerate the material of the Book of the Gospels, nor the matter of the Cross, but that which these represent. For in what respect does a cross that does not have the figure of the Lord differ from the cross that has it? It is the same in the case of the Mother of the Lord. *For the honor which is given to her is referred to Him Who was made of her incarnate.* Similarly also *the brave acts of holy (hagioi) men stir us up to become brave and zealous, to imitate their virtues, and to glorify God. For the honor that is given to the best of fellow-servants is a proof of good-will towards our common Lord, and the honor which is given to the icon passes over to the prototype.*[12] Now this is an unwritten tradition (*agraphos paradosis*), as is also the worshipping towards the East and the veneration of the Cross, and very many other things similar to these.

That the Apostles handed down much that was *un*written, the Apostle of the Gentiles says in these words: "Therefore, brethren, *stand fast, and hold the traditions* which ye have been taught, *whether by spoken word or our epistle.*"[13] And to the Corinthians he writes: "Now I praise you, brethren, that ye remember me in all things, and keep the traditions as I delivered them to you."[14]

2. THE SEVENTH ECUMENICAL SYNOD:

Concerning the Holy Icons[15]

This Holy and Ecumenical Synod, which, by the grace of God and the assent of our pious and most faithful sovereigns, Irene the new Helen, and the new Constantine, her God-guarded offspring, has assembled in this glorious metropolis of Nicaea for the second

---

12   St. Basil, *On the Forty Martyrs; Concerning the Holy Spirit*, Ch. 27.

13   2 Thessalonians 2: 15.

14   1 Corinthians 11: 2.

15   Excerpts from the decrees (*praxeis*) of the Seventh Holy, Great, Ecumenical Synod, the second of Nicaea, held in 787. I have made the translation from the ancient Greek text contained in Mansi's *Sacrorum Conciliorum Nova et Amplissima Collectio*, Florence, 1767, Vol. 13, cols. 129, 132, 377, 380.

time, having by reading understood the doctrines of our venerable
and blessed Fathers, glorifies God Himself, by Whom wisdom was
given to them for our instruction and for the formation of the
Universal (*Katholike*) and Apostolic Church. Those, however,
who do not accept their doctrines but contrive to obscure the real
truth by their innovations (*kainotomiai*), they subdue with the
Psalmist's voice: "The enemies have done wickedly in Thy holy
places! And they have boasted, saying that 'There is no more any
teacher, and there is none who will know that we distorted the
word of truth.' " [16] But we, keeping in every respect the doctrines
and ordinances of our God-inspired Fathers, proclaim with one
mouth and one heart, neither adding anything to nor taking anything from that which has been transmitted to us by them; but
these we stoutly affirm, by these we stand fast. Thus we confess,
thus we teach, as the six Holy and Ecumenical Synods have defined
and established. . . .

We salute (*aspazometha*)[17] the form of the venerable and
life-giving Cross, and the holy relics of the saints, and we receive,
salute, and kiss the holy and venerable icons, according to the
ancient tradition of the holy Universal Church of God, and of our
holy Fathers, *who both received them and determined that they
should be in all the most holy churches of God,* and in every place
of His Dominion. To these holy and venerable icons, as we have
said, we give honor (*timomen*) and salutation and *honorable
reverence* (*timetikos proskynoumen*): namely, the *icon* of the
incarnation of our great God and Savior *Jesus Christ,* and of our
immaculate Lady and all-holy *Theotokos,* of whom He was pleased
to become incarnate, that He might save us and deliver us from
every impious madness after idols; also of the incorporeal *Angels* —
since they appeared to the righteous in the form of men. Also the
forms and icons of the divine and most famed *Apostles,* of the
Prophets, who speak of God, of the victorious *Martyrs,* and of
*other Saints; in order that by their paintings we may be enabled to
rise to the remembrance and memory of the prototype, and may*

---

[16]   Psalm 73: 3–4, 9 (Septuagint).

[17]   'Saluting' an icon consists in performing such acts as bowing before it,
crossing oneself, saying a prayer, and kissing it.

partake in some measure of sanctification. These things we have been taught to hold, and have been confirmed in holding, by our holy Fathers and their divinely delivered teachings. . . .

We keep all the ecclesiastical traditions which have been handed down to us, whether written, or unwritten, free of innovations. One of the traditions which we thus preserve is that of *making representational paintings, which is in accord with the history of the preaching of the Gospel, as confirming the real and not merely the imaginary incarnation of God the Logos,*[18] *and as contributing to our good in other ways.* For those things which illustrate each other emphasize each other.

These things being so, we, as proceeding in the royal pathway, and following the divinely inspired teaching of our holy Fathers, and the tradition of the Universal Church — for we know that it is of the Holy Spirit which dwells in her — define with all exactness and care that just as the form (*typos*) of the precious and life-giving Cross, so also the venerable and holy icons, *both in painting and mosaic and other fit materials,*[19] should be set forth in the holy churches of God, on the sacred vessels and vestments, and on walls and panels of wood, both in houses and by the roads — that is, the icon of our Lord God and Savior *Jesus Christ,* of our spotless Lady the *Theotokos,* of the honorable *Angels,* and of *all Saints and Holy Men. For the more continually they are seen in*

---

[18] The representation of Christ is of special theological significance, as an affirmation of His Incarnation. To reject Christ's icon is virtually to deny His Incarnation; to accept and venerate it is to affirm and recall His Incarnation.

[19] In the Western Church, extensive use has been made of stained glass, so it was obviously assumed in the West that this is fit material for depicting sacred persons and events. But in the East, in the Orthodox Church, stained glass has not been used in iconographic decoration, apparently because Orthodox iconographers have regarded it as unsuitable, or at any rate far inferior to the mosaic and the fresco, which they used for the representation of sacred figures on the walls, domes, vaults, apses and arches. One consideration was probably the fact that icons made of stained glass, when compared with frescoes, mosaics, and panels, seem crude works, with broken up bodies, whose diverse fragments are held together by unaesthetic pieces of metal. Another important consideration was probably the fact that icons made of stained glass are non-functional during night services, when there is no light outside to illuminate them. The whole window on which the figures are depicted is then just a solid piece of blackness. It is otherwise with frescoes, mosaics, and panel icons: even the dim illumination provided by the candles and oil-burning sacred lamps renders their forms and colors visible.

*iconic form, the more are the beholders lifted up to the memory of
the prototypes and to an aspiration after them.*

To these should be given *salutation (aspasmos) and honorable
reverence (timetike proskynesis), not* indeed the *true worship (latreia) of faith, which pertains to the divine nature alone.* But in
the same way as to the form of the precious and life-giving Cross
and to the holy Book of the Gospels and to the rest of the sacred
objects, so to these also shall be offered *incense and lights,*[20] in
honor of them, according to the ancient pious custom. *For the
honor which is paid to the icon passes on to that which the icon
represents, and he who reveres the icon reveres in it the person who
is represented.* For thus the teaching of our holy Fathers, that is,
the tradition of the Universal Church, which from one end of the
earth to the other has received the Gospel, is strengthened. Thus
we follow Paul, who spoke in Christ, and the entire divine Apostolic
company and the holy Fathers, holding the traditions which we
have received.

---

20   To this day lights are offered by the Orthodox in honor of icons, both
in the church and at home. In the church, a sacred lamp (*kandeli*) is suspended
before each of the large icons on the lower part of the iconostasis, as well as
before certain others, while at home there is an ever-burning sacred lamp placed
in front of the icons that are set on a small icon stand in one of the rooms.

APPENDIX B

THE TECHNIQUES OF ICONOGRAPHY

By Photios Kontoglou

1. *Frescoes*[1]

Here, briefly, is what a fresco is and what its root is. If one has a freshly plastered wall and paints on the lime anything he wishes, using pigments mixed with water — provided these are metallic oxides — and lets the wall dry, he will see that what he painted does not come out with rubbing or washing, even though the paint was made with water, without any glue, oil, or other adhesive material. Lime has the property of keeping and fixing the color, provided the pigment is not of plant origin or chemical, because then the lime destroys it. This is the principle on which fresco painting is based.

To execute a fresco, one needs much knowledge and experience, because lime has many peculiar properties. For example, it causes the hues to change, some more and others less; and if a mistake is made it cannot be corrected. Also, the lime does not hold pigments that are applied to it after it dries, and wetting it does not help at all.

Frescoes were executed in very early times. This art was used more during the Hellenistic period, and even more during the Byzantine. In Byzantine times, superb, unsurpassed frescoes were executed. Myriads of churches, from the time of the catacombs to 1830, were decorated with frescoes.

Whoever does frescoes must be very fast and must know well what he is going to do, so as not to have to delete. He must be able

---

[1] From the articles *Technikoi Tropoi tes Zographikes* ("Techniques of Painting"), in the Athenian newspaper *Eleutheria,* February 6, 1955, and *Sta Eremokklesia* ("At the Country Chapels"), *Eleutheria,* April 3, 1955.

to endure fatigue, because he may have to work for ten or twelve hours without interruption, without eating, and without sitting. Otherwise the lime will dry up and it will be impossible to work on it.

The painter calculates how much of an area he is able to paint in a day, and plasters so much of the wall. The next day he plasters the adjacent area, uniting the new with the old plastering.

In order to paint a true fresco, the plastering must be done with lime only, without sand. A fresco done on a surface which has been covered with lime mixed with sand does not have the luminousness and wonderful color possesseed by a fresco done on plain lime.[2]

The application of the colors follows a definite system. First, the painter puts what is called in the language of iconography the *proplasmos*.[3] This is a dark color. In the case of the face and other exposed parts of the body, it is coffee-brown. Upon this he later paints lighter tones, which in the case of the face, hands and other exposed parts of the body are called *sarkomata*,[4] while in that of the garments and other objects they are called *lammata*.[5] In painting the face, a soft shadow, called *glykasmos*,[6] is painted between the *proplasmos* and the *sarka*. Finally, upon the *sarka* and *lammata* are placed what are called *psimmythies*.[7] These are thin white lines that are put on the parts that rise above others, they are the highlights.[8]

2. *Panel Icons*[9]

Another important technique of painting is with egg. This,

---

[2] In his book *Explanation of Orthodox Iconography,* Kontoglou explains that the lime should be mixed with thin straw, as the latter has the property of "retaining moisture and rendering the lime stronger" (Vol. 1, p. 52).

[3] This term is derived from *pro* = before, and *plassein* = to form. *Proplasmos* is, so to speak, the proximate matter upon which later form will be put.

[4] A word derived from *sarka* = flesh.

[5] Vittae, stripes of color.

[6] Literally, sweetening.

[7] From *psimythizein* = to paint with white lead.

[8] The system outlined in this paragraph is also employed in doing panel icons.

[9] From the article *Technikoi Tropoi tes Zographikes.*

too, seems to be very old; but it appears conspicuously in Byzantine times. The principle of this technique, like that of fresco painting, is simple. You take an egg, keep the yolk, remove its skin, put the yolk in a cup containing vinegar or water equal in volume to the yolk (vinegar prevents it from becoming putrid and gives brightness to the color), and after mixing the various pigments with this liquid they are ready to be used. If you wish, you may put the white of the egg also, but you must add a little sap from a branch of a fig-tree, in order to dissolve its strands, and thus it becomes good and firmer when it dries.

With egg, the pigments take on a rare sweetness. Also, one can do very delicate work that cannot be done with any other medium. This is why it is used in miniatures. With time, the paint becomes very strong, because the egg petrifies. The most important thing is that a painting done with egg does not become black after a long period of time, nor does the paint crack, as happens with oil colors. If the panel does not rot, the paint made with yolk is, I would say, everlasting.

This technique has been used in making the old icons that are painted on panels, and all the miniatures that are painted in old manuscript books — wonderful and priceless works.

Those panel icons which are blackened are not so because the colors have become black, but only the varnish that covers them. When someone who is skilled in cleaning icons removes the varnish the colors shine as if they were painted today. There are some panel icons which are a thousand years old, and they look as if they are made of enamel, bright and fresh.

It should be noted that paint made with egg as a medium can be used on walls, too. The old artists often finished with such paint wall paintings which they had done with the fresco technique, because the lime had dried up before they had completed them.

Another technique which was used by the old icon painters was that known as 'encaustic.' They called it thus because they painted with colors mixed with wax and placed on fire, and they spread the paint with a small heated trowel, called the *kestron*. The encaustic technique, too, produces works that are durable and pleasant to the eye. But this technique was usually employed only for small panel icons.

The old painters heated the wax, because they did not have turpentine. Today, some melt it in turpentine and proceed to paint.

Among the works that have been done with this technique are some portraits, dating from the first and second centuries A.D., that were found in Egypt. They are in an excellent state of preservation. There are also some remarkable Byzantine panel icons at the Monastery of Mount Sinai, done in the fifth, sixth, and seventh centuries.[10]

3. Mosaics[11]

The art of making mosaics is very difficult. It requires great skill and even greater patience, because the artist who wants to work with tesserae[12] has to represent whatever he wishes by placing one tessera close to another tessera. And since it is not possible to do with tesserae the delicate work that is done with the painter's brush, the artist is compelled to make his designs as far as possible simpler. The same is true of the colors — because it is not possible to mix them as does the painter, he must know in advance where each color will go, and arrange them in such a manner that they appear harmonious to an eye that looks from far off. This is why paintings that have been made with tesserae are impressive and simple, with thick lines and clear colors.

Artists who wanted to decorate a church with mosaics baked plates of glass containing different colors, each plate about a centimeter thick. They broke these plates into pieces by means of a pointed hammer, specially designed for this purpose, making them small pieces of different shapes, most of them squares like dice, and put them in boxes. For each color they made three or four shades of tesserae, ranging from the darkest to the lightest shade. Gold tesserae were made in a special way. The artists made a plate of

[10] For a fuller treatment of the subject of panel icon-painting, see Demetrios Dukas' fine, well-documented, article "The Technique of Byzantine Icon-Painting," in *The Greek Orthodox Theological Review,* Easter Issue, 1956.

[11] From the book *Taxeidia* ("Travels") Athens, 1928, p. 64.

[12] The small pieces of colored glass, marble, and the like used in making mosaics.

transparent glass, and after they glued gold leaf onto it, they covered the gold with a thin layer of transparent glass and baked it in a furnace. Then they broke it into small pieces, like the other tesserae.[13]

In order to execute the mosaics, they first covered the wall with a certain type of cement. Then the chief master would take the designs which he had drawn in advance, and would impress them onto the moist cement. Next he would hurriedly put a little color on the impressed designs. Now it was on these traces that the artists implanted the tesserae, looking at the worked out designs on paper which the chief master had given them.

The faces and the hands were executed with finer tesserae. The master artists placed the lines on the design and executed the more delicate parts of the painting, while the younger, less skillful artists filled the gold background and the garments. The chief master put the finishing touches on the face, and examined the whole mosaic, changing whatever needed correction.

---

[13] In his article *Ta Mosaika* ("Mosaics"), which appeared in *Eleutheria* in 1951, Kontoglou notes that in addition to such materials the Byzantines used natural stones.

TWO RUSSIAN BOOKS ON ICONS

1. EUGENE N. TRUBETSKOI:

Icons: Theology in Color[1]

This book consists of three essays on the Russian icon by the outstanding Russian philosopher and gifted writer Prince Evgenii Nikolaevich Trubetskoi (1863–1920) that were written before the Russian Revolution of 1917 and published as individual articles during the First World War. They have been translated from the Russian by Gertrude Vakar and are introduecd by Professor George M. A. Hanfmann (Harvard University), who also contributed an informative Appendix. The titles of these essays are "A World View in Painting," "Two Worlds in Old-Russian Icon Painting," and "Russia and Her Icons."

Trubetskoi speaks in these essays as a man of deep religious faith, as one committed to the Orthodox Christian religion, as an admirer of old-Russian icons, and as a thinker who seeks to explain the nature and meaning of authentic holy icons from a theological and philosophical standpoint.

He rejects naturalistic or, as he calls them, "realistic" icons. Realistic painting on the Western model, he says, invaded Russian churches in the seventeenth century, along with other reforms.[2] In such icons, Christ and the saints are depicted with "puffy faces," "red mouths," "thick arms," "fat thighs," and the like.[3] He remarks that *"icons must not be painted from living people,"* because "an icon is not a portrait, but a prototype of the future man-within-

---

1 New York: St. Vladimir's Press, 1973. 100 pages, 16 color prints.
2 P. 20.
3 Pp. 20–22.

the-church." [4] The aspect of the figures depicted must be unworldly, ascetic, their features refined, spiritualized.

Now old-Russian icons may appear to a superficial observer "dry and lifeless;" but "spiritual life shines through with incomparable power." [5] Again, the figures of saints give the impression of immobility. This immobility, however, "is an attribute of those images where not only the flesh but all human nature is silenced, where it no longer lives its own life but a superhuman life;" it is "the immobility of divine repose in which the saints are immersed." [6]

He who is "beguiled by the delights of the flesh" will feel repelled by the ascetic, stern images, because "to heed their call, one has to renounce a large part of his life, the part that is dominant in the world." [7] Such icons "demand that we leave behind all trivial concerns, because 'earthly concerns,' which the church enjoins us to 'lay aside,' also serve the dominance of sated flesh." [8]

Too often, remarks Trubetskoi, "the icon remains an object of superficial aesthetic enjoyment that does not penetrate to its spiritual meaning." [9] Yet its beauty is primarily spiritual. The icon is symbolic in nature; it has an otherworldly meaning. It expresses the beauty of God's design, the beauty which Dostoievsky had in mind, when he said: "Beauty will save the world." [10] "Our icon painters," adds Trubetskoi, "had seen the beauty that would save the world and immortalized it in colors." [11]

In his essay "Russia and Her Icons," the author notes the important part that was played by Greek icon painters, from the eleventh to the early part of the fifteenth century, in the iconographic decoration of Russian churches and in the development of Russian iconography. He mentions as examples Isaiah the Greek and Theophanes the Greek. The latter, he explains, "was the foremost Novgorod master and teacher of icon painting. Andrei Rublev

---

[4] P. 21.
[5] P. 22.
[6] Pp. 24, 25.
[7] P. 27.
[8] P. 28.
[9] P. 42.
[10] P. 37.
[11] *Ibid.*

[*c.* 1370–1430], the founder of independent Russian painting, was his pupil." [12]

However, Trubetskoi sees a major change in Russian iconography during the fifteenth and sixteenth centuries: it becomes Russianized. Everything in Russian icons becomes Russian: "the church architecture, even the minor details of daily life." [13] Russian traits often appear even "in the faces of the prophets, apostles, and even the Greek saints Basil the Great and John Chrysostom. Novgorod artists even dare to paint a Russian Christ." [14] According to Trubetskoi, Russian "icon painting reaches its highest perfection in the fifteenth century, shaking off foreign [i.e. Byzantine] tutelage and becoming truly original and Russian." [15]

It is the claim of Trubetskoi that in becoming Russianized the icon in Russia also became superior to the Byzantine. Thus, he sees in Russian icons of this period a "warmth of feeling" that is foreign to those done by the Greeks of Byzantium. [16] Also, he remarks that "Russian icon painting, in contrast to the Greek, did not kill the life of the human face, but gave it higher spirituality and meaning." [17] Those who have a wide acquaintance with Byzantine as well as with Russian iconography — such as was not possible in Trubetskoi's time — would grant the merits of Russian icons of the distinctively Russian period spoken of by Trubetskoi, but would not accept his thesis that these icons are superior to the Russian icons of the earlier period or to Byzantine icons outside Russia, judged from the standpoint of 'warmth' and spiritual expression. They would add that in characterizing Greek or Byzantine icons as cold and lifeless, Trubetskoi is but echoing a major misinterpretation then widespread in Western Europe, [18] with whose philosophy he was familiar. [19] Further, it should be recalled that Trubetskoi himself notes that the old-Russian icons of the distinctively Russian period of iconography,

12   P. 74

13   P. 75.

14   *Ibid.*

15   P. 79.

16   P. 24.

17   P. 24; cf. p. 58.

18   See my book *Byzantine Thought and Art,* pp. 59–60.

19   See e.g. pp. 7, 27 of his book.

which he especially esteemed, also appeared to "superficial observers" and to those "beguiled by the delights of the flesh," as immobile, lifeless, and even repellent.

Trubetskoi makes many penetrating observations about the close relationship, on the one hand between the religious fervor and loftly world-view of an age and the flourishing of a highly spiritual art, in particular architecture and icon painting, and on the other hand between the spiritual decline and the prevalence of the world-view of "biologism" in an age and the decline of its art.

His book, which is written in a clear and lively style, is important for all those who are interested in iconography, especially in Russian icons. It sets forth some key ideas for the proper understanding of the nature and meaning of authentic, traditional Orthodox icons — ideas that have been developed recently by two eminent Russian writers, Leonide Ouspensky (1902 —) and Vladimir Lossky (1903–1958). These ideas, it may be added, have been arrived at independently and been amply expounded by their Greek contemporaries Photios Kontoglou (1895–1965),[20] famous icon painter, and Panayotis A. Michelis (1903–1969),[21] eminent aesthetician.

2.   LEONIDE OUSPENSKY AND VLADIMIR LOSSKY:

The Meaning of Icons[22]

This work first appeared in a German version published in Switzerland (Bern, 1952). The present version has been made "from the original, and slightly amended Russian text of Ouspensky and French text of Lossky." [23] Ouspensky is an iconographer as well as a writer, while Lossky is best known for his writings on the mystical theology of Eastern Orthodoxy.

---

[20]   See my book *Byzantine Sacred Art,* in which I present selected writings of Kontoglou on Byzantine art.

[21]   See my book *Byzantine Thought and Art,* Ch. 5, which is devoted to a discussion of Michelis' book *An Aesthetic Approach to Byzantine Art.*

[22]   Translated by G. E. H. Palmer and E. Kadloubovsky. Boston: Boston Book Art Shop, 1955. 222 pages; 12 figures in text; 1 diagram; 59 plates, including 12 in color.

[23]   P. 8.

The volume opens with a Foreword by Titus Burckhardt. Then follows a chapter by Lossky on "Tradition and Traditions," and two chapters by Ouspensky: "The Meaning and Language of Icons" and "The Technique of Iconography." The rest of the text consists of brief sections, some by Lossky and others by Ouspensky, under the general heading "Explanation of the Main Types of Icons." The first section deals with the iconostasis, the second with the 'Holy Door' (i.e. the Beautiful Gate). The remaining fifty-seven sections deal with icons depicting Christ, the Theotokos, and other sacred persons, as well as incidents from sacred history. Interspersed throughout the text, and closely related to it, are photographs of icons (nearly all Russian) and designs for icons.

The most important parts of this work are the long chapter on the meaning and language of icons, and the sections which explain the main types of icons. The chapter on the meaning and language of icons provides a sound explanation of the general nature and function of the sacred icon, while the sections which deal with individual icons provide a more definite knowledge of the language of icons. Iconography, says Ouspensky, is a means which the Church employs to convey its teaching, to transmit the revelation of the divine world, to point to the Kingdom of Heaven. "The icon is placed on a level with the Holy Scriptures and with the cross, as one of the forms of revelation and knowledge of God." [24] The meaning of the icon "lies precisely in that it transmits, or rather testifies visually to these two realities, the reality of God and of the world, of grace and of nature. Just like the Holy Scriptures, the icon transmits historical fact, an event from Sacred History or an historical personage, depicted in his real physical form and, again like the Holy Scriptures, it indicates the revelation that is outside time, contained in a given historical reality. Thus, through the icon, as through the Holy Scriptures, we not only learn about God, but we also know God." [25]

Iconography succeeds in indicating holiness, in revealing the divine world, not merely by the theme it employs, but also by the *mode of expression*. It has established a symbolic language, which

---

[24] P. 32.
[25] P. 37.

the authors discuss. Ouspensky points out that the painting of true
icons requires spiritual experience and vision, and a living relation
with Tradition. When this experience is lacking, and the link with
Tradition has been broken, symbolical realism becomes an incompre-
hensible language for the iconographer, it is abandoned, and art
becomes secularized. Such a phenomenon, he says, occurred in Russia in the seventeenth century, when a secularization of religious
consciousness took place. Iconography began to be penetrated "by
the very principles of Western religious art, which are alien to
Orthodoxy," [26] since they call for the expression of the artist's
"personality," of his "I," rather than the expression of the objective
truth of Divine revelation. Half-worldly and even wholly-worldly
icons were the result.

Concerning the iconographer and the creation of icons, Ouspensky makes also the following important remarks. To create
genuine icons, an icon painter must live in the Tradition, must be
a member of the body of the Orthodox Church, participating continually in its sacramental life. "For a true iconographer, creation
is the way of asceticism and prayer, that is, essentially, a monastic
way." [27] Thereby "liberation from all passions and lusts of the
world and the flesh" is attained, and the human will is subjugated
to the will of God.[28] It follows that the true icon painter "works
not for himself, not for his own glory, but for the glory of God.
Therefore an icon is never signed." [29]

The last statement needs explanation. What is meant is not that
the true iconographer never puts his name on an icon, but that he
never puts his name on it all by itself, or with expressions such as
"Work of," or "Made by." He either does not record his name at
all, or if he does, he always writes it after the phrase "Through the
hand of" (in Greek, *Dia cheiros*), or "Hand of" (*Cheir*). The
reason for this is that he feels that a Divine element enters into the
execution of his icon, that Divine grace illumines his mind and
guides his hand.[30]

---

[26] P. 49.
[27] P. 43.
[28] Pp. 43–44.
[29] P. 43.
[30] See also my *Byzantine Sacred Art*, p. 69.

The treatment of iconography in *The Meaning of Icons,* taken as whole, constitutes a valuable contribution to the subject, and should be welcomed both by the Orthodox who desire to deepen their understanding of this aspect of their religion, and by others who are interested in iconography.

BIBLIOGRAPHY

Cavarnos, Constantine, comp., ed., and trans., *Byzantine Sacred Art*. New York, 1957.

Cavarnos, Constantine, *Anchored in God: Life, Art, and Thought on the Holy Mountain of Athos*. Athens, 1959; Belmont, Massachusetts, 1975.

Cavarnos, Constantine, *Byzantine Thought and Art*. Belmont, 1968, 1974.

Damascene, St. John, *Ekdosis Akribes tes Orthodoxou Pisteos* ("An Exact Exposition of the Orthodox Faith"), Migne, *Patrologia Graeca*, Vol. 94.

Damascene, St. John, *Pros tous Diaballontas tas Hagias Eikonas* ("Against Those Who Decry the Holy Icons"), Migne, *Patrologia Graeca*, Vol. 94.

Dionysios of Fourna, *Hermeneia tes Zographikes Technes* ("Explanation of the Art of Painting"), ed. by A. Papadopoulos-Kerameus. Petroupolis (Petrograd), 1909.

Dukas, Demetrios, "The Technique of Byzantine Icon-Painting," *The Greek Orthodox Theological Review*, Vol. II, No. 1 (Easter Issue, 1956).

Grabar, Andre, *Byzantine Painting*. Geneva, 1953.

Kontoglou, Photios, *Ekphrasis tes Orthodoxou Eikonographias* ("Explanation of Orthodox Iconography"). 2 vols. Athens, 1960.

Michelis, Panayotis A., *Aisthetike Theorese tes Byzantines Technes* ("An Aesthetic Approach to Byzantine Art"). Athens, 1946, 1972.

Michelis, Panayotis A., *An Aesthetic Approach to Byzantine Art*. With a Foreword by Sir Herbert Read. London, 1955, 1965.

Ouspensky, Leonide, *L'Icone: Vision du monde spirituel; quelques mots sur son sens dogmatique*. Paris, 1948.

Ouspensky, Leonide, and Vladimir Lossky, *The Meaning of Icons,*
    translated by G. E. H. Palmer and E. Kadloubovsky. Boston,
    1955.

Rice, David Talbot, *The Beginnings of Christian Art.* London, 1957.

Rice, David Talbot, *Art of the Byzantine Era.* New York, 1963.

Soteriou, Georgios A., *Christianike kai Byzantine Archaiologia*
    ("Christian and Byzantine Archaeology"). Athens, 1942, 1962.

Soteriou, Georgios A., *Eikones tes Mones Sina* ("Icons of the Mon-
    astery of Sinai"). 2 vols. Athens, 1956–1958.

Trubetskoi, Eugene N., *Icons: Theology in Color,* translated by
    Gertrude Vakar. New York, 1973.

Xyngopoulos, Andreas, *Schediasma Historias tes Threskeutikes
    Zographikes Meta ten Halosin* ("Sketch of the History of Re-
    ligious Painting After the Fall of Constantinople"). Athens,
    1957.

INDEX

INDEX

Alexandria, 13

anagogic nature of icons, 32, 36-37, 38, 52-53

anatomy, 19, 21, 38, 39

angels, 14, 25, 26, 28, 52, 53, Plates 11, 15, 18, 23

Annunciation, 23, Plate 2

Antony the Great, St., 47

apostles, 13, 23, 32, 36, 45, 52, Frontispiece, Plates 2, 9, 12

apse, main eastern, 24, 26-27, 35, Plate 3

apses, 15, 53

archangels Michael and Gabriel, 23, 27

archetypes, 36, 39

Arnabassi, 17

arrangement of the icons in a church, 15, 23-29

Asia Minor, 14, 17

Athanasios the Great, St., 46; representation of, 28

Athens, 16, 18, Plates 3, 10, 11

Athos, Mount, 16, 17, 19, 20
   Church of the Protaton, 19, Plates 8, 21
   Monastery of Iviron, Plate 15
   Monastery of Lavra, main church and refectory of, 20, Plate 24
   mosaics, 16
   panel icons, 16, Plate 8
   wall paintings, 17, 19, Plates 21, 24

Attica, 17

Augustine, St., 40

Balkans, 14, 19, 20

Baouit, 17

Baptism, 23, 24, Plate 15

Barlaam, martyr, 13

Basil the Great, St., 13, 31, 33-34, 40, 49, 51; representations of, 28, 62

bas-reliefs, 22

Beautiful Gate, 22-23, 64, Plate 2

beauty:
   physical, 21, 38, 39, 41, 45
   spiritual, 30-31, 34, 38, 39, 40-48, 61
   the Archetypal, 41, 45, 46

bema, 22, 28

bemothyra, 23, Plate 2

Boiana, 17

Bulgaria, 14, 17, 21

Byzantine Empire, Byzantium, 14, 15, 16, 17, 18, 19, 20, 35, 62

Byzantine Guide to Painting, 29

Byzantine iconography, 14, 18, 20-21, 36-48, 55, 62

Byzantine Museum at Athens, 18

Cappadocia, 17

catacombs, 13, 16-17, 55

Christ, representations of, 13, 16, 22-24, 27-28, 32, 33, 35, 36, 49, 50, 52, 53, 60, 62, 64, Plates 2, 3, 4, 5, 6, 10, 11, 14, 15, 16, 17

Christian Iconography, 29

Constantine, Byzantine Emperor (eighth century), 51

71

Constantinople, 14, 15, 16, 19, 20, 31
  Church of Hagia Sophia, 15-16, 44
  Church of the Monastery of Chora (Kahrie Djami), 15-16, 19
Cretan School of iconography, 18, 20, Plate 24
Crete, 18, 20
cross, 15, 23, 35, 38, 51, 52, 53, 54, 64, Plate 2
Crucifixion, 23, 24, 32, 37-38, 51, Plates 2, 16
Crusades, 16, 18
cubism, 39
Curtea de Arges, 17
Cyprus, Plate 14

Daniel, Book of, 28
Daphni, Church of, 15-16, Plate 10
David the Prophet-king, 14, 27, 52; representation of, 26
Demetrios, St., 43
Descartes, 40
Despotikai ('Sovereign') icons, 22-23, Plates 2, 4, 5, 6, 7
Didron, Adolphe N., 29
Dionysios of Fourna, 29, 67
distortion, 14, 37, 39
Dodekaorton, 23, 24, Plates 14, 15, 16, 17, 18
dome, central, 24-26, 27, 35, Plates 10, 11
Dorotheos, Abba, 46
Dostoievsky, 61
Dragalevici, 17
Dukas, Demetrios, viii, 58, 67, Plates 12, 13
Dura, 17
Durand, Paul, 29

Egypt, 17, 58

eikon, 13, 49
Ekphrasis, 29, 67
Elijah, representation of, 26
encaustic technique, 57-58
Euthymios, St., Plate 24
evangelists, representations of, 24, 26, Frontispiece, Plates 11, 13
Explanation of Orthodox Iconography, 29, 56, 68
Explanation of the Art of Painting, 29, 67
expressionism
  of Orthodox iconography, 14, 19, 37, 64-65
  of recent art, 39

faith, Christian, 14, 30, 31
Festivals ('Feasts') the Twelve Great, 23, 24, Plates 14, 15, 16, 17, 18
frescoes, 16, 17, 18, 19, 20, 28, 29, 53, 55-56, 57, Plates 18, 19, 21, 22, 24
functions of icons, 30-35, 49-54, 64

Gabriel, Archangel, 23, 27
George, the Great Martyr, 43, Plate 20
glykasmos, 56
Glykophilousa, Plate 5
God, 23-24, 25, 26, 27, 31, 33, 34, 40-41, 43-49, 50, 52, 61, 64, 65
Gospels, 23, 24, 26, 27, 28, 51, 53, 54
Grabar, Andre, 37, 67
Gracanica, 17
Greece, 14, 15, 16, 17, 18, 20 ,21
Greek Church Fathers, 31, 33, 36, 40, 41-42, 44, 45, 47, 53, 54
Greek icon painters, 18, 19, 20-21, 61, 62

Gregory Nazianzen, or the Theologian, St., representation of, 28

Gregory of Nyssa, St., 14, 40-41, 46-47

Grunewald, Mathias, 37-38

Habakkuk, representation of, 26

Hagia Sophia, Church of, at Constantinople, 15, 16, 44

halo, 24, 42

Hanfmann, George M. A., 60

Hellenistic art, 18, 55

Hierarchs, the Great, representation of, 28, Plate 2

Hodegetria, Plate 4

Holy Communion, representation of, 28

Hosios Lukas, Church of, 15-16, Plates 16, 17

hymnography and iconography, 25, 26, 27, 30, 33, 34, 41

icon, meaning of the term, 13

Iconoclasm, 13, 15, 16, 17, 29, 32, 34-35

iconographer, 13, 14, 36, 37, 38-40, 55-56, 58, 61, 65

iconostasis, 16, 22-24, 26, 64, Plate 2

Icons: Theology in Color, 60-63

idealism of Byzantine iconography, 14, 18, 19

idolatry, 34, 50

idols, 34, 50, 52

Irene, Byzantine Empress, 51

Isaac, icon of the sacrifice of, 14

Isaiah, representation of, 26

Isaiah the Greek, icon painter, 61

Italy, 14, 20-21

Jeremiah, representation of, 26, Plate 12

John Chrysostom, St., 13-14, 40; representation of, 28, 62

John Climacos, St., 37, 43, 44

John Damascene, St., 13-14, 31, 32, 33, 34-35, 40, 49-51, 67

John the Evangelist, or the Theologian, 23, 26, 45; representation of, 38, Frontispiece, Plate 11

John the Forerunner, or the Baptist, representations of, 23, 24, 25-26, 28, 36, Plates 2, 8

Kahrie Djami, 15-16, 19

Kalotino, 17

Kastoria, 17

Kataphygiotis, Kallistos, 47

Kontoglou, Photios, 21, 29, 36, 38, 55-59, 63, 67, Plates 3, 5, 11, 18

lammata, 56

Leibniz, 40

Leo the Isaurian, Emperor, 34

Leo VI, the Philosopher and Emperor, 44

Liturgy, the Divine, and iconography, 25, 27-28

Lossky, Vladimir, 37, 63-66, 68

Luke, the Evangelist, representation of, 26, Plates 11, 13

Macedonia, 18, 19

Macedonian School of iconography, 18-20, Plate 21

Mango, Cyril, 15, 31

Mansi, 51

Mark the Ascetic, St., 43

Mark the Evangelist, representation of, 26, Plate 11

martyrs, 13, 28, 31, 32, 33, 34, 43, 52, Plates 19, 20

Matthew the Evangelist, representation of, 26, Plate 11

Maximos the Confessor, 40, 42

Meteora, 17, 20, Plate 2

Michael, Archangel, 23, 27

Michelis, P. A., 37, 63, 67
Milesevo, 17
miniature icons
　in manuscripts, 57, Frontis-
　　piece, Plate 15
　mosaic, 16
mosaics, 15-16, 17, 18, 19, 22, 24,
　28, 44, 53, 58-59, Plates 4, 10,
　12, 13, 16, 17
Moscow, 18, Plate 23
Moses, 43, 49; representation of,
　26
music, sacred, and icons, 33, 34
Mystra, 17, 19, 20
　Church of Aphentiko or Bron-
　　tocheiou, 19, Plate 19
　Church of St. Demetrios, 19
　Church of Pantanassa, 19
Mytilene, Plates 6, 20

Nagoricino, 19
narthex, 28
Nativity, 23, 24, Plate 14
naturalism, 21, 39, 60
Nea Moni, Church of the Mon-
　astery of , 15-16
Nerezi, Church of, 17
Nicaea, 51
Nilos the Ascetic, St., 43
Novgorod, 17, 18, 61, 62

Ochrida, 17
oil colors, 21, 57
Old Testament, 26, 28, 49-50
Ouspensky, Leonide, 36, 37, 63-
　65, 67-68

Palmer, G. E. H., 63, 68
Painter's Guide, 29, 68
Panagia, 16; see also Theotokos
panel icons, 15, 16, 17-18, 19, 20,
　22, 29, 53, 56-68, Plates 1, 2,
　4, 5, 6, 7, 8, 9, 20, 23

technique of painting, 17, 56-
　58
Pantocrator, icon of Christ as,
　24-25, 27, 36, Plates 6, 10
Panselinos, Manuel, icon painter,
　19, Plate 21
Patmos, Frontispiece
Paul the Apostle, 24-25, 51, 54
　representations of, 13, 36, 45,
　　Plate 9
pendentives, 24, 26, Plates 11, 13
perspective, 21, 37, 38
Peter the Apostle, representation
　of, 45
Peter the Great, Czar, 20
Photios, Patriarch of Constanti-
　nople, 15, 31, 32
Picasso, 39
Plato, 40, 41
Platytera, icon of the Theotokos
　as, 24, 26-27, Plate 3
Plotinos, 40
Prochoros, St., Frontispiece
prophets, 24, 25, 26, 32, 52,
　Plates 12, 21
proplasmos, 56
proskynetarion, 22, 33, Plate 1
prothesis, 28
psimmythies, 56

Raphael, 38
Ravenna,
　Baptistery of the Orthodox, 15
　Mausoleum of Galla Placidia,
　　15
　Sant' Apollinare in Classe, 15
　Sant' Apollinare Nuovo, 15
　San Vitale, 15
Read, Herbert, 39, 67
realism, 60, 65; see also natural-
　ism
　symbolical, 65
Renaissance painting, 38, 39
Resurrection, 23, 24, Plate 17

Revelation, Book of, 25, 26, 28
Rice, David Talbot, 68
Romans, 15
Rome, 13, 15, 17
    Church of Santa Maria Anti-
    qua, 17
    Church of St. Cosmas and Da-
    mian, 15
Rublev, Andrew, icon painter,
    18, 61-62, Plates 9, 23
Rumania, 14, 17, 21
Russia, 14, 17, 20, 21, 22, 60-65
Russian icon painters, 18, 20,
    61-62, 63, 65, Plates 9, 23
Russian icons, 60-65, Plates 9, 23

Sacrifice of Isaac, 14
saints, 24, 28, 29, 32, 33-34, 37,
    43, 49, 51, 52, 53, 61
saluting of icons, 22, 33, 52, 53,
    54
sanctification through icons, 30,
    33, 39, 52-53
Saqqara, 17
sarka, 56
sarkomata, 56
Savvas, St., Plate 24
Scripture and iconography, 13,
    23, 25, 26, 28, 49-50, 64
sculpture, 22, 50
Serbia, 19, 21; *see* also Yugo-
    slavia
Seventh Ecumenical Synod, 32-
    33, 49, 51-54
signing of icons, 65
Sinai, Mount, 58, 68, Plate 4
Slavic countries, 18
Sofia, 17
Solomon, representation of, 26
Sopocani, 17
Soteriou, George A., 27, 68
stained glass, 53
statues, 22
Stethatos, Niketas, 30

Stokes, Margaret, 29
Studenitza, Plate 22
symbolism, 13, 27, 30, 31, 32, 33,
    34, 39, 42, 44, 47, 61, 64-65
symbols, 13, 15, 26, 34, 35
Symeon Nemanya, St., Plate 22
Symeon the New Theologian,
    St., 30, 40, 47
Syria, 14, 17

techniques of iconography, 17,
    55-59, 64, 67
tempera, 17, 21, 56-57
The Meaning of Icons, 63-66, 68
Theophanes the Cretan, icon
    painter, 20, Plate 24
Theophanes the Greek, icon
    painter, 18, 61
Theotokos, 16, 22-23, 24, 25, 26-
    27, 28, 32, 33, 36, 38, 49, 51,
    52, 53, Plates 2, 3, 4, 5, 11, 14,
    16, 18
Thessaloniki, 15, 19
    Church of Hagia Sophia, 15
    Church of Hosios David, 15
    Church of St. Demetrios, 15,
    19
    Church of St. George, 15
    Church of the Holy Apostles,
    15-16, 19
tradition and iconography, 27,
    34, 51-54, 65
Tretiakov Gallery, 18, Plate 23
Trubetskoi, Eugene N., 60-63, 68
Turks, Ottoman, 16, 19

United States, 16, 21, Plates, 12,
    13

vaults, 15, 24, 28, 53
veneration of icons, 22, 32-35,
    49-54; distinguished from wor-
    ship, 33-34, 51-52, 54
Vinci, Leonardo da, 38

Virgin, the All-Holy (*Panagia*),
 see Theotokos
Vladimir, 17

wall paintings, 15, 16-17, 18, 19,
 20, 22, 24, 28, 53, 57, Plates 3,
 14; *see* also frescoes
Western art, 20-21, 29, 37, 38,
 60, 65

Whitehead, Alfred North, 40
worship, icons as a means of, 30,
 33-35, 49-54

Xyngopoulos, Andreas, 68

Yugoslavia, 14, 17, 19, Plate 22

Zacharias, Prophet, Plate 21